To Bethany

May the Lord bless and watch over you + your family. Please get to know God's armor + then wear it daily.

Love and Best Wishes
Uncle Dan

ARMOR OF GOD

PREPARING FOR BATTLE

DANIEL BOEHM

WestBow Press®
A DIVISION OF THOMAS NELSON
& ZONDERVAN

Copyright © 2017 Daniel Boehm.

All rights reserved. No part of this book may be used or reproduced by any means, graphic, electronic, or mechanical, including photocopying, recording, taping or by any information storage retrieval system without the written permission of the author except in the case of brief quotations embodied in critical articles and reviews.

WestBow Press books may be ordered through booksellers or by contacting:

WestBow Press
A Division of Thomas Nelson & Zondervan
1663 Liberty Drive
Bloomington, IN 47403
www.westbowpress.com
1 (866) 928-1240

Because of the dynamic nature of the Internet, any web addresses or links contained in this book may have changed since publication and may no longer be valid. The views expressed in this work are solely those of the author and do not necessarily reflect the views of the publisher, and the publisher hereby disclaims any responsibility for them.

Any people depicted in stock imagery provided by Thinkstock are models, and such images are being used for illustrative purposes only. Certain stock imagery © Thinkstock.

ISBN: 978-1-5127-7709-3 (sc)
ISBN: 978-1-5127-7710-9 (hc)
ISBN: 978-1-5127-7708-6 (e)

Library of Congress Control Number: 2017903029

Print information available on the last page.

WestBow Press rev. date: 03/10/2017

Contents

Dedication vii
Acknowledgments ix
Preface xi
Prelude xiii

Armor of God 1
Sandals of Peace 11
Belt of Truth 23
Breastplate of Righteousness 32
Helmet of Salvation 41
Shield of Faith 52
Sword of the Spirit 63

Review 73
Conclusions 79
Prayer in the Spirit 83
The Warrior's Shield Defined 91
About the Author 99

Dedication

This study guide on the armor of God was a request by Lance Yoshikawa, one of the members in our men's Bible study group. We were getting ready to complete our latest topic, so I requested suggestions for our next study.

I did a lot of research online about the armor of God but had very little luck in finding a good study guide for our group, so I proceeded to do more research, thereby compiling the knowledge needed to attempt to write this guide. Now I can't really take the credit for the study, since the Holy Spirit seemed to take the lead and fill me with what I can only call inspired passion. He put words and feelings into my head and heart until eventually this study was completed.

So this study is dedicated to the men of my Bible study group whose desire it is to change their environment by changing their mind-set and to further the word of God through their words and actions. These men strive to change their lives so that they may bring glory to God on a daily basis by standing firm and bringing God into their daily activities.

Thank you for your patience, E.B.C.'s Panera men's Bible study group in Maplewood, Minnesota.

Acknowledgments

I would like to thank and give mention to the resources that I've used to compile this study. Without these wonderful Christian authors, this study would not have turned out the way it has. So thank you one and all.

Each of these websites was used by the Holy Spirit to inspire me to move on with the course of the study.

Berit Kjos: allaboutgod.com. All were published by AllAboutGOD.com Ministries, M. Houdmann, P. Matthews-Rose, R. Niles, editors, 2002–2014. Used by permission.

Rev. Marsh Hudson-Knapp, First Congregational Church of Fair Haven UCC.

Philip Paul Sacco, *Awaken the Warrior.*

Dean VanDruff

Bibles referenced are King James, New King James, Gospel Literature Services, New American Standard, New Revised Standard, Weymouth, and the most used, New International Version.

The Holy Spirit provided me with inspiration from the heart. The greatest thanks is to the Holy Spirit, who inspired me throughout the research, writing, and compilation of all parts of this study; for giving me the design and definition of the Warrior's Shield as a symbol for the armor of God; and finally, for getting me off my duff through hearing messages about completing what one has started. If it is a gift and you don't share it, then you are wasting it and not passing on blessings.

Preface

Thank you to Lance Yoshikawa, whose idea it was to do a study on the armor of God. Lance had a strong desire to understand what Paul was talking about in Ephesians 6:11: "Put on the full armor of God, so that you may be able to stand against the wiles of the devil." It was his suggestion and zeal that compelled me to do the research, compile the information, and put my heart and head into making it something that would help our group grow in the service to our Lord Jesus Christ.

As I compiled this, through research on the work of others whose hearts were in the same place as my own, I found myself using examples from my own life experiences. Since the change of heart that has taken place in me as I study God's word and the life of my Lord and Savior Jesus Christ, I continue to long to serve my Lord in a manner that will help to bring others into the light of Christ Jesus. So I believe that the Holy Spirit has been guiding my thoughts and leading me to further what others have started in a way that will help my brothers in Christ to become not only followers but leaders and warriors in the battle that sometimes rages unbidden in our thoughts.

I believe this study has helped each of us to become closer to the heart of Jesus, who through his sacrifice gave us life eternal. Only through the blood of Christ could we have been saved, and now it is our turn to do our part to help bring others into the light of his salvation. I believe that once you put on the armor of God, you have made a commitment to serve others as he served us, out of love, and with the heart of a warrior, we will be able to stand on the truth of God's word and lead by actions and go where others fear to tread.

"I have given you authority to trample on snakes and scorpions and to overcome all the power of the enemy; nothing will harm you" (Luke 10:19).

In this study, I requested that all participants design a shield that would represent who they were and where they stood in the battle for our minds and lives. So having asked them to do this, I as the group leader also designed a shield that would represent my heart and soul. So one weekend, I sat down with my computer, prayed for guidance, and thereby sought to do what I requested of the others.

I opened up AutoCAD 14 and began; mind you, I was a novice at using this system, so when things started to come together and form this shield, I was rather amazed at what transpired.

The design of the shield and the definition of the meaning of each part of the shield can only be called an inspiration because the design just flowed onto the paper, and when it was completed I thought to myself, *Where did this come from?* Then another unction came over me: to come up with an explanation of what each part of the shield stood for, and somewhere along the line, the placement of each item came into play. Again, this all flowed from my head to my heart through my hand, onto the paper, and the results became the Warrior's Shield Defined.

Note: Some of the questions throughout the study have example answers, whereas others do not. The reasoning behind giving my answers to some of the questions is simply this: I hope that being transparent with you will help readers be open and honest with themselves.

Prelude

"When you are about to go into battle, the priest shall come forward and address the army. He shall say: 'Hear, O Israel, today you are going into battle against your enemies. Do not be fainthearted or afraid; do not be terrified or give way to panic before them. For the Lord your God is the one who goes with you to fight for you against your enemies to give you victory'" (Deuteronomy 20:2–4).

The same God that was spoken of and prayed to back then is the same God we speak of and worship today. He is unchanging, forever loving, all knowing, and all powerful. He always was and always will be. He is the alpha and the omega, the giver of life and the preserver of our souls. He is our heavenly Father, who has forgiven us our sins through the blood of his Son Jesus, and he will stand with us in this battle against the darkness of despair, for despair is the tool of the enemy: Satan himself.

When you go into battle against your enemies, do not be fainthearted or afraid; do not be terrified or give way to panic before them. For the Lord your God is the one who goes with you to fight for you against the enemy, to give you victory. This is the way I believe we should look at our spiritual battle, which is for the minds and hearts of not just ourselves but everyone. As you go forth, wearing the armor of God, know that he is with you to be your guide and to strengthen you in all things. Far too often, we go forth into battle for our very souls and do so unwittingly, for this battle is there on a daily basis in our everyday lives, and we must go forth with the Holy Spirit bolstering us so that we can stand, stand not only for ourselves but for those who cannot stand for themselves. The word of the Lord is our protection and our weapon, so arm yourselves with scripture and faith; take the promise of God, embrace it, and do not fear.

Too often, we look at ourselves and see only our weaknesses and ugliness, so we don't see how we can be a blessing or help to others. We don't see the forgiveness and love our Father in heaven has given us through his Son Jesus. Moses only saw his personal weakness, yet God used him to bring the Israelites out of Egypt. So who are we to say that he cannot use us for his glory? "The Lord said to him, 'Who gave man his mouth? Who makes him deaf or mute? Who gives him sight or makes him blind? Is it not I, the Lord? Now go; I will help you speak and will teach you what to say'" (Exodus 4:11–12).

In this book, we will learn that wearing God's armor daily will protect us, and it will also open our eyes to the world around us. He will give us what we need to bring his word and love to those around us. We are the shepherds to his sheep, and it is up to us to protect them from the enemy: the wolves in sheep's clothing and demons that seek to tear and destroy through lies and deceit, misdirection, and false witness. The enemy is all around us, and it is up to us to see through his charade and bring light to those lost in the darkness of fear, anger, hurt, and ignorance.

"After this, the word of the Lord came to Abram in a vision: 'Do not be afraid, Abram. I am your shield, your very great reward'" (Genesis 15:1).

God is our shield, protector, confidant, and Lord. He will surely strengthen those who stand for his truth, protect the weak, love their neighbors, and forgive those who know not what they are doing, for they do not know the Lord our God or his Son Jesus or the Holy Spirit who dwells in those who love him and have accepted the gift of salvation through the death and resurrection of Jesus. This is who stands with us: we the willing who are united in the family of Christ and who choose to wear the armor of God and do battle with the dark. Injustice is the cloak of the enemy; lies and deceit are his weapons of choice. He is armored in loathing and shielded with contempt, and he wears a helmet of bigotry.

"So justice is driven back, and righteousness stands at a distance; truth has stumbled in the streets, honesty cannot enter. Truth is nowhere to be found, and whoever shuns evil becomes a prey. The LORD looked and was displeased that there was no justice. He saw that there was no one; he was appalled that there was no one to intervene; so his own arm achieved salvation for him, and his own righteousness sustained him. He put on righteousness as his breastplate, and the helmet of salvation on his head; he put on the garments of vengeance and wrapped himself in zeal as in a cloak. According to what they have done, so will he repay wrath to his enemies and retribution to his foes; he will repay the islands their due" (Isaiah 59:14–18).

So don the armor of God and wrap yourself in the cloak of zeal, for these are the trappings of a warrior equipped for battle. Then go forth in the knowledge that if God will bring you to it, God will see you through it. He will bring to light what is hidden in darkness and will expose the motives of the heart.

Are You Ready for Action?

For me, I know what this means: that into my life will come attacks, blessings, changes, and challenges, at times all at once or in uneven masses.

My way is clear, my sword is sharp for the enemy, and I am prepared for change to occur; I am ready to move forward to serve and to defend and to reap the blessings. When you are at the forefront of the battle lines, it can be lonely place, yet if you are willing, the rewards are plentiful for the few who stand to open the way for others to follow.

Know this: Unless you are willing to get into the game, get off the bench, and step off the sidelines and are prepared to get dirty, stinky, and sweaty; get knocked down; and get back up again, skinned up and maybe a bit bloody and bruised, you will always be lukewarm and never able to stand or become a warrior, for no warrior ever learned the art of war from just a book; no swordsman ever defeated an enemy without hours of practice, resulting in a lot of cuts and bruises.

I have no time for the complacent and no patience for whiners; I do have words for the worthy, hands of healing for the hurt, and power for the warriors of God's army. We are entering the age of the warrior, the new hero and leader, who is prepared to go forth into the world of sin and corruption, knowing that God is with him to guide him along the way. You can change the world if you will but change your life and positively affect those in your circle of influence, be it large or small.

Look for ways to add the practical principles of God's word found in the Bible to the way you live your life on a daily basis. The only way the benefits of God's armor will be manifested in your life is to put on the whole armor, which is the character of Christ, himself. "I know the plans I have for you," declares the Lord, "plans to prosper you and not to harm you, plans to give you hope and a future" (Jeremiah 29:11).

How would you describe the mettle of Jesus: docile, a pacifist, a rebel, a revolutionist, an activist, or what – some would say?

- He was docile as a sheep before its shearers – for he was totally yielded to His Father's Plan.
- He was a pacifist – for He was able but did not call upon the legions of warring angels that were at His command
- He was a rebel – not against His Father but against the self-righteous religious rulers.
- He was a revolutionist – the revolution continues to this day where history is still in the making.
- He was an activist – for He dedicated His life to righting social wrongs.
- He was the perfect Servant Leader who taught by both His words and actions.

To get the ball rolling on the first topic of discussion, the mettle of the warrior, I'd like to ask you a question:

How would you describe the mettle of Jesus: docile, a pacifist, rebel, revolutionist, activist, or what?

_____
_____
_____
_____

AUTHOR'S EXAMPLE:
Docile: Yes, as he was led from the garden of Gethsemane to stand before Pilot, he went willingly; as he was tortured, he fought not; when they put him on the cross, he lay down his life. For us, he died.

Pacifist: Yes, in the garden after his betrayal and Peter lopped the ear off a soldier, Jesus admonished him; in his parables, he talks about turning the other cheek, and if a man steals your sandals, give him your cloak also.

Rebel: Yes, he would hang out and eat with the undesirables in society.

Revolutionist: Yes, he spoke out against what the Pharisees and Sadducees were teaching as formalized religion.

Activist: Yes, he would heal the sick and challenge the Pharisees' beliefs and teachings. He led the apostles in the ways of truth and sent them out amongst the masses to convert others, and he chased the moneychangers and profiteers out of the temple.

He was the living incarnation of God: the creator of all things, a warrior for the people, a servant to some, and a king to all.

We most often describe him as the Lamb of God, but what about his moniker as Lion of Judah? How do you see him fitting those descriptions?

_____
_____
_____
_____

AUTHOR'S EXAMPLE: The Lion laid down with the Lamb; as a Lion, he was strength, the leader, and the teacher. As the Lamb, he was the sacrifice, and he laid down his life for us all.

As he is our perfect model of character, are you prepared to compare yourself to his mettle?

_____
_____
_____
_____

AUTHOR'S EXAMPLE: I fail to compare, but I strive to emulate his character by being truthful, showing compassion, loving, serving, and leading in his teachings. Attempting to walk the path before me fully armored, prepared to stand in place of those who cannot or will not stand up for themselves. To forgive and be forgiven, for my sins are great, and only through the grace of God am I able to change my life and become a warrior for Christ Jesus. By trying to lead a life that shows whose I am, for I am a child of God, the son of the King, and a warrior in the army of light.

And lastly, when you realize that you are called to action, are you willing to take action? Have you found your place on the sidelines of the spiritual war that we are all embroiled in, or are you looking to make your way to the front?

_____
_____
_____
_____

AUTHOR'S EXAMPLE: I am willing to go where he sends me, but until the call comes, I will be learning and preparing others and myself for the inevitable battle. I have served on the sidelines, waiting until the marching orders called me to the forefront of the battle. But now, I have realized that the battle is here and the battle is now; the clarion call has sounded, calling us to arms. The time is now; pick up your weapons of war and go forth with the protection only afforded by the armor of God and the word of God, to him shall be the honor and glory.

Father God, the battle is upon us, and we are yet ill prepared to stand on our own, much less to stand for others. So as we complete this study, I pray that you will open our minds to your full blessings that you have given us through your Son Jesus, and that this knowledge will not only lead us but show us how to become leaders and warriors for you on this earthly realm, where Satan holds sway. So Lord, we seek your divine guidance as we delve into this study of truth and perseverance. Amen.

Armor of God

What Is the Full Armor of God?

The phrase "full armor of God" comes from a passage in the New Testament: "Therefore put on the full armor of God, so that when the day of evil comes, you may be able to stand your ground, and after you have done everything, to stand. Stand firm then, with the belt of truth buckled around your waist, with the breastplate of righteousness in place, and with your feet fitted with the readiness that comes from the gospel of peace. In addition to all this, take up the shield of faith, with which you can extinguish all the flaming arrows of the evil one. Take the helmet of salvation and the sword of the Spirit, which is the word of God" (Ephesians 6:13–17).

Let's examine the things that cause Christians to stumble or fall down in their Christian walk (or faith). A specific list of these things does not exist; however, the Bible provides insight into this area, starting in the book of Genesis and ending with Revelation. Instead of discussing a list of things that make Christians fall, let's instead examine where the battleground is found. With this knowledge, we can better prepare ourselves to "stand firm" against the schemes of the devil.

Where is this battleground?

DANIEL BOEHM

Understanding that the spiritual battleground for humankind is found within the mind, this battleground is critical, especially for Christians who think they are covered in a blanket of protection, not realizing that they are now main targets of the enemy.

What does this statement mean to you: "You can't fight a battle if you don't know where it is"?

_____
_____
_____
_____

Author's example: To me that would be like fighting shadows in the dark. What I mean is that if you don't know that your mind is the battlefront, trying to fight this battle would be like fighting blindfolded: not knowing where the enemy is, what he is attacking you with, or from which direction he is coming.

Controlling the messages we think to ourselves (self-talk) is where the fiercest spiritual battles occur, and the average Christian doesn't even know it. Now, if this battle is so hard for Christians, then is this not even more true for non-Christians, who are oblivious to the war waging around them? The devil is a master at subterfuge and will start with something small to distract you from spiritual thoughts; then you are back in his element, where he can lead you astray. Redirection of thought and distraction are used to destroy the good thought path and any thoughts of God's truth. How could this pattern be realized in everyday life?

_____
_____
_____
_____

Author's example: How often are you in a great, meaningful conversation with someone and just as you are getting ready to make your key biblical point, the phone rings, a waiter comes to take your order, or someone interrupts to ask you a perfectly innocent question? Look for this happening to your meaningful conversations, and you will see it occur all too often. Open your eyes to the battle and realize you are a victim of spiritual warfare, and the battle is for the mind and thoughts of humans.

Next time this occurs to you, stop and focus heavily on your key point. Keep repeating it in your mind so you don't forget, and as soon as the interruption is over, immediately bring the conversation back up and share your thoughts: "As I was saying ..."

When you doubt yourself, thinking that you can't do something, you will always be right—and you won't do anything. (Read *What Do You Say when You Talk to Yourself* to get a better understanding of self-talk.) So when you find yourself getting distracted from your worthwhile goals by what may be trivial tasks, refocus on what is really important and not distracting.

What kind of distractions could this be for you?

_____
_____
_____

You must become spiritually mobile and spiritually agile in order to protect, guard, and defend your most vulnerable areas of personal weakness (the old sin nature, temptations, and areas you struggle in daily). The key point as a Christian is to wrap your mind in God's truth and surround yourself with the Scriptures (not your own humanistic or personal truth).

What could these truths be?

_____
_____
_____

Author's example: I used to think that I was not good enough to deserve good things in this life, but the truth is that I am a son of God, and therefore I am good enough for whatever blessings life has to offer or God wants to give me.

You are surrounded by a world that operates on hard facts. The spiritual side of life seems so unreal in this age of megabytes and cell phones, yet its existence is very much a reality. The armor of God is activated in your life through prayer. Pray on each piece of the armor during your daily devotional time, and apply its truth to your specific situation. In addition, use the armor to activate God's power all day long as you encounter the battles of life.

Author's note: Since I have been praying on the armor on a daily basis, I have found that God does strengthen my self-control through my actions and thoughts. He is always there to lend me the help I need to refocus my thoughts when my mind becomes lost or in turmoil. Because I have on the helmet of salvation, I know that God is in the forefront of my mind at all times; all I have to do is ask, and he is there.

Paul tells us to complete our preparations by praying in the Spirit. Let the Holy Spirit lead you in worshipping God. Pray also for others, that all of God's people may stand strong and faithful in the armor of God.

Who in the Old Testament is a prime example of moving forward into the jaws of death, armored only in God's armor?

_____
_____
_____
_____

Author's example: David when he stood up to Goliath. Prior to the face-off, he was dressed in battle armor from King Saul, but the armor was too cumbersome, so he removed it and went out to meet his destiny with only a sling and some stones for weapons. His true armor was the word of God, which David believed was the truth, and therefore he feared not the giant Philistine.

Ephesians 6:11 says we all recall the story of David, the youngest son of Jesse, and the giant named Goliath. If someone killed Goliath, then the Philistines would be their servants. But if Goliath killed their man, then they would all be servants of the Philistines.

Who now represents the modern-day Philistines?
_____
_____
_____
_____

Author's example: I believe it is anyone who is trying to take God out of our lives—from schools, public view, or military worship—and all other forms of suppression of the word of God.

Well, David wasn't afraid of Goliath; his father, Jesse, had sent him to the battle, and he obeyed. But Eliab, the oldest of David's brothers, got angry that David came to the battle. Others laughed at such a small young boy coming to kill the huge, nine-foot giant, who dwarfed him not only in stature but in knowledge and experience in warfare. But the stature of the giant didn't upset David, for God was his backing/covering, and he had a covenant with God. The uncircumcised Philistine had no covenant.

Saul gave David the okay to go after the giant and said God would watch over him. But he also wanted David to put on the armor of a soldier. But David had never tried the armor, and he felt it just wasn't for him. So he took his staff, his sling, and five stones and went to the battle.

DANIEL BOEHM

How was David armed with the "armor of God"?

_____
_____
_____
_____

Author's example: His faith was in his Lord; he had confidence in whose he was, not who he was. He went forth in belief that the Spirit was with him; David put his whole trust in the Lord, as in Psalm 23:4: "Yea, though I walk through the valley of the shadow of death, I will fear no evil: for thou art with me; thy rod and thy staff they comfort me."

David knew whom he served. He preferred to put his whole trust in God, not in man's armor. He gave God the glory before the battle. He began to speak faith and not self-righteousness like Goliath, who after that encounter never spoke again. David loaded a stone into the pocket of his sling and hurled it at the giant, and it struck Goliath in the head, knocking him down to the dirt of the earth. Then David went to the giant, and using Goliath's own sword, he severed the head of this giant, ending the Philistine reign of terror.

Like David, we must don the armor of God and face the adversary, not allowing the enemy to intimidate us and get the upper hand.

Heavenly Father, help us to be bold and put our full trust in you to take us through the rough waters of life, through the battles that we face each day with the enemy. Help us to know that you and you alone are the one who will keep us against all the wiles of the devil, if only we place our trust in you. Help us to know you in the fullness of your power, to know that you are the alpha and the omega and that nothing on earth or in between will keep us, as you will, to protect us in this present world. I pray that each of us put on the true armor of God, arming ourselves with truth in order to stand until your return. We give you the glory, honor, and praise due your name. In Jesus's name, we pray. Amen.

To begin the study, let's review some Scripture verses from both Old and New Testaments that will help in the understanding of the study; some talk about the actual armor that was worn to protect the body, while others talk about the armor in a figurative sense. This is what most of the study is about: wearing the armor without actually putting on each piece (which could become cumbersome).

The equipment of a soldier is discussed in Jeremiah 46:3-4 and Ephesians 6:14-17.

Figurative aspects are in Romans 13:12, 2 Corinthians 6:7 and 10:4, Ephesians 6:11-17, 1 Thessalonians 5:8, and 1 Corinthians 14:8 (GLT): "For if a trumpet gives an uncertain sound, who will get himself ready for war?"

Luke 21:36 (NIV) says, "Be always on the watch, and pray that you may be able to escape all that is about to happen, and that you may be able to stand before the Son of Man."

Malachi 3:2 (NAS) says, "But who can endure the day of His coming? And who can stand when He appears?"

1 Corinthians 10:12-13 (NIV) says, "So, if you think you are standing firm, be careful that you don't fall! No temptation has seized you except what is common to man. And God is faithful; He will not let you be tempted beyond what you can bear. But when you are tempted, He will also provide a way out so that you can *stand up* under it."

What does this verse mean or say to you?
_____
_____
_____

AUTHOR'S EXAMPLE: To me, this means that God will always give me what I need to overcome any and all obstacles in life, if only I allow him to take the lead in my life. In order to do this, I must become less and allow God to become more, as well as realize that sometimes life just gets in the way, and sometimes God just says no. These times do not mean that God is not with me, only that sometimes adversities are brought into my life to teach me and help me to grow.

"But to Him who is able to keep you safe from stumbling, and cause you to stand in the presence of His glory free from blemish and full of exultant joy" (Jude 1:24 Wey).

"Submit therefore to God. Resist the devil and he will flee from you" (James 4:7 NAS).

"Be on your guard; stand firm in the faith; be men of courage; be strong" (1 Corinthians 16:13 NIV).

"Be empowered by grace in Christ Jesus" (2 Timothy 2:1 GLT).

"I was made a minister according to the gift of the grace of God given to me, according to the working of His power" (Ephesians 3:7 GLT).

"And God is able to make all grace abound to you, so that in all things at all times, having all that you need, you will abound in every good work" (2 Corinthians 9:8 NIV).

"Since His power is so glorious, may you be strengthened with strength of every kind, and be prepared" (Colossians 1:11 Wey).

"I can do all things through Him who strengthens me" (Philippians 4:13 NAS).

God's armor brings victory because it is far more than a protective covering. It is the very life of Jesus Christ himself. "Put on the armor of light," Paul wrote in his letter to the Romans. "Clothe yourselves with the Lord Jesus Christ" (Romans 13:12,

14). When you do, he becomes your hiding place and shelter in the storm, just as he was to David. Hidden in him, you can count on his victory, for he not only covers you as a shield, he also fills you with his life. "I am the vine: you are the branches," said Jesus. "If a man abides in Me and I in him, he will bear much fruit: apart from me you can do nothing" (John 15:5).

Since living in the safety of the armor means oneness with Jesus, we can expect to share his struggles as well as his peace. Remember: God has promised us victory in the midst of trials, not immunity from pain. So "do not be surprised at the painful trial you are suffering, as though something strange were happening to you, but rejoice that you participate in the sufferings of Christ" (1 Peter 4:12-13). Christian heroes who have been tortured for their faith continue to testify to the supernatural strength, even joy, that enables them to endure unthinkable pain, as affirmed with Paul in Romans 8:37-39. (A good book by Richard Wurmbrand, *Tortured for Christ,* gives testimony of acts of heroism lived out by Christians under communistic dictatorship.)

This wonderful truth has become reality to all who believe and follow Jesus. When you put on his armor, his life surrounds you, keeping you safe, close to him, and free to be his precious friend and trusted companion. So "put on the Armor of Christ" (Ephesians 6:14-17). He is your victory.

How Do You "Put on" God's Armor?

This life in Christ begins with learning, affirming, and trusting in each part of the armor. Truth: God's revelation of all that he is to us, all that he has done for us, and all that he promises to do, his enduring truth, is written in the Bible, revealed by the Holy Spirit, and realized through Jesus Christ. It cuts through all the world's distortions, deceptions, and compromises. When you study, memorize it, live it, and follow its truth, it enables you to see the world from God's high vantage point. Putting on the first piece of the armor means feeding on the truth through daily Bible reading and making it part of yourself.

Can you relate past experiences to spiritual attacks?
___
___
___
___

Are you presently fighting one now?
___
___
___
___

List some spiritual battles we all must face at some point in life:
___
___
___
___

Which of these would be your greatest battle?
___

What steps are you taking to combat and overcome this battle?
___
___
___
___

So let us begin by learning about the first piece of armor every warrior must start with.

Sandals of Peace

"And your feet fitted with the readiness that comes from the gospel of peace" (Ephesians 6:15).

Feet Fitted with the Readiness: That wherever you may go, you will be available to be used as an instrument of peace. So exhale fully and breathe in the peace of God. Invite the Holy Spirit to show you anyone with whom you need to be reconciled. Forgive them and seek their forgiveness.

How to Forgive
By an Unknown Author

"One day a while back, a man, his heart heavy with grief, was walking in the woods. As he thought about his life this day, he knew many things were not right. His very soul was filled with anger, resentment and frustration."

To avoid copyright infringement, I will not put this entire story into these pages, so I ask that you go to www.thewarriorsshield.com. Go to the bottom right of the web page and click on the Read More button at the bottom of How to Forgive; read this poem about forgiveness that will bring you to your knees if you put yourself in the man's place.

DANIEL BOEHM

This is a short story about a man who has gone through many struggles in life, some so hurtful that to even think about forgiving them seems to make him ill, or at least too upset to think straight. It is about him having a conversation with Jesus, where he is telling Jesus all that has transpired to bring him to such straits, and he tells the Lord how he just can't forgive some of the people who have brought pain and suffering into his life. He is hurting so deeply that before he knows it, he is kneeling at the foot of the cross upon which the body of Christ is hanging, and then the Lord speaks to him.

This, my friends, is the part that all must read, for if you stop and think about it and put yourself in this man's place, what do you think the Lord would say to you? I believe the words spoken to this man could be the same words that the Lord would say to each one of us, yet when he would say it to you and to me, it would cover our own personal questions, hurt feelings, and disappointments that are presently troubling our souls.

So remember that even though it may be hard to see how you're going to get through something, when you look back in life, you realize how true this statement is. Read the following line slowly, and let it sink in:

If God brings you to it, he will bring you through it.

As you begin your study with the sandals of peace, acknowledge that without God in your life, you could not have peace. The "peace that transcends all understanding" (Philippians 4:7) is available to you only as you give your life entirely over to his control. As you strap on your sandals each day, give your cares and concerns to him, and ask him to carry them. God's peace will be left in their place.

Father God, help me to prepare myself for the rigors of life, which include putting my life on the line for your glory. Help me to properly don the sandals of peace, by lacing them tightly to my feet and ankles to keep my steps sure and sound. Prevent me from the pitfalls of life that the enemy places before me.

Know the truth about God.

Embrace the Christian paradigm, which says our inner peace and readiness is through our union and ongoing relationship with Jesus Christ (Romans 5:1; Ephesians 2:14; John 14:27, 16:33, and 20:21).

Beware of, recognize, and resist the world paradigm that teaches peace through occult practices and union with cosmic forces or nature spirits.

What does peace mean for or to you?
_____
_____
_____

AUTHOR'S EXAMPLE: For me, it means the ability to go to bed at night with no regrets, knowing that I did all that I could to live my life for God. Does this mean that I have peace on a nightly basis? No, rather it is very seldom that I go to bed with peace in my heart because I know I have not truly been the best me I could be. I have been selfish rather than selfless. I have slacked, doing nothing where I should have done something. I have judged others according to the world view rather than as a fellow child of God. I thought about who I am and what is best for me, and if I do something for you, what will you do for me? What has happened is I have forgotten whose I am. I am only able to sleep at night by receiving grace through the reading of God's word before I go to sleep.

Without his sandals, a soldier would not be prepared to fight and could be easily defeated. Paul tells us that our preparation for battle is the gospel (good news) of Jesus' life, death, and resurrection. The work of Jesus here on earth brought us peace with God. This reconciliation through Jesus allows us to fight with boldness, confidence, perseverance, and peace.

The fiery darts of the enemy are not always thrown or cast through the air; rather they are land mines designed to trip you up and cause you to let down your guard. The gospel is like a map that shows the land mines marked with a big red X, so that you can walk around or step over some of these mines or even step on them without getting crippled.

What are some of these crippling obstacles that have been lying in your path, waiting for you to stumble over in your life?

_____
_____
_____
_____

AUTHOR'S EXAMPLE: Mine used to be pornography. I would walk through a store and be drawn to the magazine racks to see what I could see as I went past, like a junkie looking to find a fix. I would watch porn on the Internet, looking for something to excite me, while my wife was sleeping alone in our bed. I used to enjoy smoking pot so it could bring me into a euphoric awareness as a way to escape the realities of life. At times, I sought refuge in a bottle of alcohol as means of numbing or postponing the pain I perceived as life.

Sandals were worn by soldiers to protect the feet from dangerous obstacles, which were disguised and left in the road or pathway to injure the feet of a soldier. This was done in order to cripple the soldier and take not only him but other soldiers out of action. This part of the armor signifies that with the preparation of the gospel of peace, you are protected against some of the common pitfalls placed in your path to divert you from the truth.

Stand in the peace of God. "Allow the peace of God to rule in our hearts" (Colossians 3:15). "Be still and know that I AM God" (Psalm 46:10). "Do not be anxious about anything, but in everything, by prayer and petition, with thanksgiving, present your requests to God. And the peace of God which transcends all understanding will guard your hearts and minds in Christ Jesus" (Philippians 4:6–7).

Be ready to be reconciled with those with whom you are in conflict. Jesus teaches, "Agree quickly with your adversary" (Matthew 5:26). Don't accept false guilt, but look courageously within yourself for the truth of any accusation and confess it. Be quick to ask forgiveness, to give it, and to seek healing for hurts in yourself and others. "Happy are the peacemakers for they shall be called the sons and daughters of God" (Matthew 5:9).

Battle shoes could be used to identify the "readiness" that comes from the gospel of peace. It's important for you to understand exactly what Paul was talking about so you can fully engage your faith when putting on your battle shoes. The Amplified translation of Ephesians 6:15 is helpful: "And having shod your feet in preparation (to face the enemy with the firm-footed stability, the promptness, and the readiness produced by the good news) of the Gospel of peace."

Let's explore the footwear analogy. When going to work, play, exercise, or relax, you usually put something on your feet that is appropriate. Each type of shoe provides a unique combination of benefits for the activity you're intending to do. Specifically, footwear provides protection, support, traction, performance, and comfort.

Footwear also bolsters your stamina to perform whatever activity you're going to do. For example, if you are going running on a hot day, you won't last long on the hot asphalt without shoes. With shoes on, you can run on that asphalt much longer.

Envision Jesus giving you new shoes so you can stand solidly and also run swiftly to meet others in peace. Now imagine putting the shoes on your feet.

Would you feel different? If so, how?
_____
_____
_____
_____

Now imagine yourself standing barefooted in a sandy and rocky terrain, like in the Middle East. You could move ever so carefully from one place to another, but without shoes on in a battle, you would be useless.

What is the correlation here between spiritual sandals and physical shoes?
_____
_____
_____
_____

Now think about this: Walking without shoes by itself can pose a problem, as we previously discussed, but with the additional weight of the other pieces of armor, it would be impossible to stand much less walk or fight in a battle. This armor would only make your feet more sensitive; they would have no protection. You would be a sitting duck for the enemy, as you would have no agility and wince in pain every time you attempted to move. This is why it is essential to have our "feet shod with the gospel of peace," for peace is the only footwear that can support you in a spiritual battle.

The spiritual footwear that comes from the gospel of peace gives you the firm-footed stability, promptness, and readiness you'll need to face your agile adversaries. The term "gospel of peace" refers to the peace you have with God through Jesus: "Therefore, since we have been justified through faith, we have peace with God through our Lord Jesus Christ, through whom we have gained access by faith into this grace in which we now stand. And we rejoice in the hope of the glory of God" (Romans 5:1–2 NIV). (Other verses on your peace with God through Christ are found in: Isaiah 53:5, Colossians 1:20, and Ephesians 2:13–22.)

Since you have gained access to God through this peace, you can use his resources to fight the spiritual battles you face. Therefore, the gospel of peace extends your "battlefield endurance" by connecting you with God's protection, support, guidance, and comfort at all times through the Holy Spirit.

Even though your faith in Jesus secures your peace with God, you often don't feel that peace. It may even seem like God is not with you. In such times, it is helpful to remember that you put the whole armor of God on by faith. Faith is the substance of things hoped for, the evidence of things not seen (Hebrews 11:1). You can't see your peace with God, but you believe you have it because God's word says you have it. When you confess that you are putting on the battle shoes (and the rest of the armor), you are speaking them on in faith. Here is an example prayer to do so:

I shod my feet with the preparation of the gospel of peace. I have peace with God through my faith in Jesus through whom I have access to God. Through the Holy Spirit, I have his resources at my disposal for the battles I may face today, so Father, please guide my footsteps and secure me on your path of righteousness today. Thank you, Father.

DANIEL BOEHM

The Bible is the reference book for the gospel of peace, so you must learn God's word. By studying the Bible and even memorizing key scripture passages, you will establish a foundation in the gospel of peace. You will be less likely to slip off God's path of truth. You will be firmly standing in good shoes. The psalmist declared in Psalm 119:165 (NKJV), "Great peace have those who love Your law, and nothing causes them to stumble."

"Your feet fitted with the readiness that comes from the gospel of peace" (Ephesians 6:15 NIV).

"As well as the shoes of the Good News of peace, a firm foundation for your feet" (Ephesians 6:15 Wey).

"As it is written, 'How beautiful are the feet of them that preach the gospel of peace, and bring glad tidings of good things!'" (Romans 10:15 KJV).

"But let me recall to you, brethren, the Good News [Gospel] which I brought you, which you accepted, and on which you are *standing*, through which also you are obtaining salvation, if you bear in mind the words in which I proclaimed it—unless indeed your faith has been unreal from the very first ... — that *Christ died* for our sins in accordance with the Scriptures; that He was *buried*; that He *rose to life* again on the third day in accordance with the Scriptures" (1 Corinthians 15:1–4 Wey).

"Beloved, I urge you as aliens and strangers to abstain from fleshly lusts which wage war against the soul." (1 Peter 2:11 NAS).

"But I say, *walk* by the Spirit, and you will not carry out the desire of the flesh. For the flesh sets its desire against the Spirit, and the Spirit against the flesh; for these are in opposition to one another, so that you may not do the things that you please" (Galatians 5:16–17 NAS)

"For those who are according to the flesh set their minds on the things of the flesh, but those who are according to the Spirit, the things of the Spirit. ... the mind set on the flesh is hostile toward God; for it does not subject itself to the law of God, for it is not even able to do so, and those who are *in the flesh* cannot please God ... But if the Spirit of Him who raised Jesus from the dead dwells in you, He who raised Christ Jesus from the dead will also give life to your mortal bodies through His Spirit who dwells in you. So then, brethren, we are under obligation, not to the flesh, to live according to the flesh—for if you are living according to the flesh, you must die; but if by the Spirit you are putting to death the deeds of the body, you will live" (Romans 8:5–13 NAS).

"Therefore my people will know my name; therefore in that day they will know that it is I who foretold it. Yes, it is I. How beautiful on the mountains are the feet of those who bring good news, who proclaim peace, who bring good tidings, who proclaim salvation [Yeshua, Jesus!] who say to Zion, 'Your God reigns!'" (Isaiah 52:6–7 NIV).

Don't be anxious about anything. Take all your needs and concerns to God in prayer: The devil will try to steal your peace, using the cares of the world, the desire for riches, fear, and any other tool to get your mind off of God. If you give in and begin to worry and get anxious about things, you'll lose the protection that comes with God's peace. Paul wrote, "Do not be anxious about anything, but in everything, by prayer and petition, with thanksgiving, present your requests to God. And the peace of God, which transcends all understanding, will guard your hearts and your minds in Christ Jesus" (Philippians 4:6–7 NIV).

This is the gospel as we have received it. It is foolishness to many, but life and light to those who believe in it and are willing to follow and be included in Christ's death. In practice, the gospel means we are dead to our self-life, with all of its lusts and instincts, and alive with new life in Christ. The good news is that by considering ourselves "dead men" in Christ, we can be put at peace with God in Christ. If we have truly died to self, then over time, our instincts will be dead to the rocks and glass and thorns of this world, which used to move us. Those standing on the gospel will not react in the flesh. Instead, we will move by God's Spirit with a protected disregard for such "fleshly" considerations, being readied by the shoes of the "death, burial, and resurrection of Christ," which is the gospel that brings peace.

Remember: The enemy will always try to convince you that you are undeserving. So give yourself permission to be human. We all fall down at various times in our lives, but it doesn't matter how many times you fall down. It only matters how many times you get back up. We all have a past, where we all have done things we are not proud of. Forget the past; God already forgave you. You can be a new creature and have victory; the exciting part is that God can use those lessons from the past to help others, if you let Him.

Thank you for the peace you give me by your grace when I trust and follow you. Show me how to help others find and receive your grace so they too can experience this peace.

On my feet, I put the shoes of the gospel. Father, prepare me by helping me to know Jesus in a deeper way. Let your work become the guiding light for every step I take today, and let the knowledge of the good news of Jesus' death and resurrection be my source of peace (Romans 5:1).

How many gates to your mind do you have that will allow Satan means of entrance?

_____
_____
_____
_____

AUTHOR'S EXAMPLE: I believe there are three major gates: two are entrances and one is an exit, but they all have equal responsibility for the securement of your mind. The eye gate allows all that you see to go directly to the mind and possibly imprint on your memory. The ear gate allows all that you hear to also enter into your mind to imprint on your memory and even to possibly confirm what you have just seen. Then there is the mouth gate; this can be the worst, for whatever comes out of it can reaffirm what the mind tells you. What I mean by this is, there are things the ears have heard that others have said that may have maligned your character, rather than edifying you. So the things you speak, your ears do hear, and these also may have negative connotations (e.g., "I am such an idiot," "I am not very smart," "I am so forgetful," "I can't do it," etc.). Also, the mouth can say things that will hurt others, even if this was not your intent. The mouth is the one gate that can be both hurtful and self-destructive, making this one of Satan's favorite gates to enter through deceit. Once you are distracted, you are defeated.

Father God, every day, help me to remember to put on your armor. I need this armor to protect my mind from things that are not of you, I need it to guard my heart from acting on emotions rather than with your Spirit, I daily need it to remind myself that I am a child of yours and that I do not serve Satan anymore. I need the armor to be an instrument of peace and not react with my old nature. When those fiery darts start flying, I need your armor to shield myself from them. Lord, let your words speak through me to those in darkness, penetrating the enemy and crushing his plans. In Jesus' name, Amen.

What are some of the land mines you face today?
_____
_____
_____

What are some of the land mines you face each day?
_____
_____
_____

DANIEL BOEHM

What could it look like going into battle wearing the sandals of peace?
_____
_____
_____
_____

What does this mean: "Grace and forgiveness go hand in hand"?
_____
_____
_____

Belt of Truth

"Stand therefore, having girded your waist with truth" (Ephesians 6:14).

Belt of Truth: "That you may be reminded that you are a child of Christ" and "He is in control" of your life.

The belt was foundational for battle. In short, it supported the weapons that allowed the soldier to fight. The belt is a reminder that Jesus is the foundation for spiritual battle. He is the truth that stands against the lies and deception of Satan. "Jesus is the way and the truth," the very basis for life. To win your spiritual battles, your fight must be anchored to the truth found in Jesus alone.

How are the belt and Jesus alike as foundations for battle?
_____
_____
_____

AUTHOR'S EXAMPLE: The belt both then and now is the foundational piece that was used to carry your equipment and weapons. You couldn't go into battle without these and expect to last long. Jesus' word being the truth in all things carries the sword of the spirit that is the foundation of the word of God, without which you won't last long in battle.

Know the truth about God.

Embrace the Christian paradigm that says: know and affirm his sovereignty, love, wisdom, and holiness (Deuteronomy 4:39; Psalms 23:1, 18:1–3).

Beware of, recognize, and resist world paradigms that teach pantheism (the worship of all gods of different creeds, cults, or peoples indifferently, a doctrine that equates God with the forces and laws of the universe), monism (a view that there is only one kind of ultimate substance, that reality is one unitary organic whole with no independent parts), or polytheism (there are many gods and goddesses).

In your words, what are these world paradigms?
_____
_____
_____
_____

AUTHOR'S EXAMPLE: With belief and worship of all gods, and a reality that is one unitary organic whole with no independent parts, and that reality is all intertwined with cosmic forces. This means that there is no one true being or creator. All is coincidence, therefore, we are all beings without a true direction in life, without a divine creator but with multitudes of gods to choose from, as we so desire. It means that we are lost.

The belt was used to hold the garment in place, to keep the soldier from getting entangled in it as he charged into battle as well as someplace for him to carry his weapons. Symbolic: Jeremiah 13:1–11; Acts 21:11; and Revelation 15:6.

Figuratively: Genesis 30:8, 32:24–25; Isaiah 11:5; and Ephesians 6:12.

ARMOR OF GOD

God's word promises "you will know the truth and the truth shall set you free" (John 8:32).

What is one truth about you that relates to the above scripture?
_____
_____
_____

AUTHOR'S EXAMPLE: That since I've become a Christian, my heart has softened to many things that before I would have rejected as being unmanly. So now that I know whose I am, I don't believe in the deceptions or lies that the world uses to characterize things as manly.

Invite Jesus to show you the truth about yourself, both beautiful and ugly. You need not fear what others say, if you know the truth about yourself. The evil one and the world are filled with deceptions. Pray for the gift of the Spirit to discern what is true about others and the world (1 John 4:1-2). Ask God's grace to know and to believe and to speak and to live only the truth. Envision Jesus wrapping a wide, pure white belt around your waist: the belt of truth.

How will this help you in your daily walk?
_____
_____
_____

AUTHOR'S EXAMPLE: I no longer feel that I have to live up to other people's standards; God made me who I am, and what I need to do is be the best me that I can. This means to be truthful in my words and actions, not having to deceive someone into thinking I am something I am not. Also to be able to discern truth in what others say about me or someone else.

"Fasten the belt of truth around your waist" (Ephesians 6:14 NRS).

"Righteousness will be his belt and faithfulness the sash round his waist" (Isaiah 11:5 NIV).

"This is how you are to eat it [the Passover lamb]: with your cloak tucked into your *belt,* your *sandals on your feet* and your staff in your hand" (Exodus 12:11 NIV).

What is meant by Exodus 12:11, and how does the belt serve you?
___
___
___
___

AUTHOR'S EXAMPLE: During the time of the Passover, the Israelites were preparing to leave Egypt, so they were to eat while being prepared to leave at a moment's notice, and as discussed previously, the belt is essential to fast movement in battle or otherwise; always be prepared.

"The power of the Lord came upon Elijah and, tucking his cloak into his belt, he ran ahead of Ahab all the way to Jezreel" (1 Kings 18:46 NIV).

"Therefore, put away lying, 'Let each one of you speak truth with his neighbor'" (Ephesians 4:25 NKJ).

"God is spirit, and his worshippers must worship in spirit and in truth" (John 4:24 NIV).

"But now you must rid yourselves of all such things as these: anger, rage, malice, slander and filthy language from your lips. *Do not lie* to each other, since you have taken off your old self with its practices and have put on the new self, which is being renewed in knowledge in the image of its Creator" (Colossians 3:8–10 NIV).

How can this be done?

_____
_____
_____
_____

AUTHOR'S EXAMPLE: By daily getting into the word so that the word can get into you. By making and reading affirmation cards. Changing the way you self-talk will change the way you talk about others. Remember: You are a sons and daughters of God, so see yourself, as royalty for God is King; therefore, his children are princes and princesses.

"They perish because they refused to love the truth and so be saved" (2 Thessalonians 2:10 NIV).

A Christian's survival in the world requires a firm grounding in the absolute truth of the Bible. The power of truth is that it sets us free by breaking the power of the devil's lies and the deception they create (John 8:31–32). Just as with Eve in Eden, the devil downplays the consequences of sin and promotes its pleasures.

How have you downplayed the consequences of sin?

_____
_____
_____
_____

AUTHOR'S EXAMPLE: By telling myself it was just that one time, or I'm not as bad as some are. It feels so good, how can it be bad, and so on. Only by becoming firmly rooted in the truth, we are best equipped to recognize the lies, resist the devil, and do God's will.

Paul mentioned that the "belt of truth" is part of the whole armor of God in Ephesians 6:14. Soldiers in Paul's day wore belts to secure their clothing and hold weapons. The belt of truth has similar but expanded functions for spiritual warfare:

Sanctification: The belt of truth sets us apart from people who don't follow God. Jesus prayed that God would sanctify us by the truth (the word): "Sanctify them by the truth; your word is truth" (John 17:17 NIV). "To sanctify" means to set apart for a special purpose and to purify. The truth helps you to stay on mission for God and avoid falling back into sin's corruption.

Guidance: The Holy Spirit uses the truth to guide you in whatever circumstances you are in. John wrote, "But when he, the Spirit of truth, comes, he will guide you to all truth. He will not speak on his own; he will speak only what he hears, and he will tell you what is yet to come" (John 16:13 NIV). Just as communications are crucial on the physical battlefield, so is the Holy Spirit's guidance via truth on the spiritual battlefield.

Intelligence and Discernment: Intelligence data and its interpretation (i.e., discernment) can play a critical role in the outcome of military conflicts. God's word reveals the truth, which helps you decisively recognize the devil's lies in spiritual conflicts. Hebrews 4:12 (NIV) explains how the word reveals the truth: "For the word of God is living and active. Sharper than any double-edged sword, it penetrates even to dividing soul and spirit, joints and marrow; it judges the thoughts and attitudes of the heart." Armed with the truth of the word, you'll recognize the devil's lies for what they are.

Battle Readiness: Belts were used in biblical times to secure loose garments so that a person could run or fight effectively (1 Kings 18:46; 2 Kings 4:29). The belt also provided a place to attach weapons (2 Samuel 20:8). When the enemy attacks you, you may have to move quickly and use your spiritual weapons (praise, prayer, sword of the spirit, etc.) on the run. The belt of truth enables you to move quickly and confidently, without tripping into lies or losing your weapons.

Putting on the Belt Each Day

You can take these key actions to securely put on your belt of truth each day:

Speak It: When you say you are putting on the belt of truth and believe it, the belt's function is maximized. Example words to speak: "I put on the belt of truth. I believe that God's word is truth, and I fill my mind with God's word. I have the Holy Spirit living in me, who will guide me in truth. The truth enables me to discern the devil's lies and avoid being taken captive to do his will."

Study the Word: Daily Bible study will help keep the truth in the forefront of your mind (John 17:17). This is done by studying the Bible, memorizing scriptures, and speaking verses applicable to the situations you face each day. Jesus said, "If you abide in My word, you are My disciples indeed. And you shall know the truth and the truth shall make you free" (John 8:31–32 NKJV). There is no substitute for Bible study during your quiet time with God. It's essential if you hope to grow closer to God and maintain victory over your old sinful habits.

Ask God to Remind You of the Truth: The Holy Spirit, the "Spirit of Truth," will remind you of the truth and guide you in truth as you walk with God (John 14:17, 26). In order for the Spirit to remind you of God's word, you have to have already read it or heard it. If you've done your part in abiding in God's word, you'll have maximum sensitivity to the Holy Spirit. You can pray this simple invitational prayer:

"Heavenly Father, please remind me of your word today and guide me in truth by the Holy Spirit. Please help me hear, know, and obey your voice in every situation. Please strengthen my ability to retain and recall your work as it applies to the situations I face. Thank you, heavenly Father. In Jesus' name I pray, Amen."

Maintaining the Belt

To keep your belt of truth in great shape, you must keep your hearts pliable and obedient to God by clinging to his word. Your belt can become corrupted by the sin you commit and tolerate in your life. For example, Joab's belt was stained by his murders of Abner and Amasa in 1 Kings 2:5.

When you give sin a protected place in your life, you embrace the lies that the sin is based on. These lies are what corrupt your belt of truth. If you sin, you must return to God in repentance, and the blood of Jesus will wash away the stains from your sins (1 John 1:7).

Thank you, my Lord, for showing me the truth about yourself. Thank you for reminding me that you are the only God, the Creator of heaven and earth, the King of the universe, my Father who loves me, and my Shepherd who leads me. You are my wisdom, my counselor, my hope, and my strength. You are everything I need each day.

Around my waist, I put the belt of truth. Father, I commit myself to Jesus as the foundation of my life today. With your strength, Lord, I will resist the temptation to stand on any worldly foundation. Jesus, you alone are my foundation for any situation that will arise today (John 14:6).

We have all lied at one time or another, so look back on it here tonight and reflect on what you have learned about lying (whether it was lies you told or were told to you).

ARMOR OF GOD

Can actions sometimes be looked upon as lies or lying?

Is withholding complete truth lying?

Are there different levels of lies, and if so, what is the difference?

Breastplate of Righteousness

"Stand firm then, with the belt of truth buckled around your waist, with the breastplate of righteousness in place" (Ephesians 6:14).

Breastplate of Righteousness: For "the protection of your emotions and your heart," so that you will be able to respond spiritually, not emotionally.

What is the difference between an emotional and spiritual response?
_____
_____
_____

AUTHOR'S EXAMPLE: An emotional response is one that is made through reaction, a spontaneous response that often puts oneself in a position of doing something that is often regrettable, whereas a spiritual response uses the wisdom that we glean through study of the Bible and the way Jesus would handle trials or opportunities that came his way.

The function of the breastplate was simple: to protect the soldier's vital organs. In close combat, the breastplate was essential for survival. It was able to deflect most direct and indirect blows to the body by an enemy soldier. No trained soldier would venture into battle without it.

How is a breastplate functional in spiritual battle?
___
___
___
___

AUTHOR'S EXAMPLE: If we went into battle against an armed and armored soldier armed with only a sword and nothing else, we would get cut, stabbed, and probably killed. Going into a spiritual battle without armor, the enemy would strike us with weapons (e.g., temptations of all kinds that could lead us to sin). And as the Bible tells us, sin is death, so without the righteousness of God through the blood of Christ, we would be naked before a killer.

Without God's armor, it would be like you were still expecting your works and your behavior to get you into heaven. It wouldn't happen. So if you start to believe that your own righteousness, effort, or good works can make you worthy of God's protection, the advantage quickly changes to benefit your enemy. Your righteousness is worthless in the battle. You need to get your eyes off of yourself and back on the provision of the cross and the righteousness that is found in a relationship with Jesus.

Know the truth about God.

Embrace the Christian paradigm that says Jesus Christ and his blood cleanses you from sin. The cross frees you from bondage to selfish nature (Psalm 100:3; Romans 3:23–24, 6:23; Galatians 2:20–21; and Philippians 3:8–10).

Beware of, recognize, and resist the world paradigm that teaches natural goodness, connectedness, and sacredness of all life.

What are these paradigms lacking?
___
___
___
___

AUTHOR'S EXAMPLE: These are missing God; they are misleading in that there is no basis for salvation or spiritual support in feelings or beliefs other than the belief in the truth of the word of God.

The breastplate was the main body armor for soldiery (Revelation 9:9–17).

Figurative: Isaiah 59:17, Ephesians 6:14, and 1 Thessalonians 5:8.

A right relationship with God (righteousness) begins with repentance. When sin is working in your life, you are being separated from God. Confess any sin (1 John 1:8–9) and any trust you have placed in getting right by being good enough (Ephesians 2:8–9). Claim Jesus' blood to wash away every sin and make you right with God. Invite Jesus to make you into his likeness (Romans 8:29). Focus on letting Jesus fill you with his light and goodness, pushing out anything else. Envision Jesus filling your body with light, starting as a small spark in your chest and working its way to become a radiant armor all about you, and at the center is a shining breastplate around your chest.

"Not having a righteousness of my own that comes from the law, but one that comes through faith in Christ, the righteousness from God based on faith" (Philippians 3:9 NRS).

"Then His own arm brought salvation to Him, and His righteousness upheld Him. He put on righteousness like a breastplate, and a helmet of salvation on His head" (Isaiah 59:16–17 NAS).

"Fashion a breast-piece for making decisions … Make it like the ephod" (Exodus 28:15 NIV).

"So give your servant a discerning heart to govern your people and to distinguish between right and wrong" (1 Kings 3:9 NIV).

"Judgment will again be founded on righteousness, and all the upright in heart will follow it" (Psalm 94:15 NIV).

"He holds victory in store for the upright, he is a shield to those whose walk is blameless, for he guards the course of the just and protects the way of his faithful ones. Then you will understand what is right and just and fair—every good path" (Proverbs 2:7–8 NIV).

Righteousness

1. In a broad sense, this is defined as the state of people who are as they ought to be; righteousness is the condition acceptable to God.
   - the doctrine concerning the way in which people may attain a state approved of by God
   - integrity, virtue, purity of life, rightness, correctness of thinking, feeling, and acting
2. In a narrower sense, justice or the virtue that gives each his due.

The part of the definition I'd like to emphasize is the "condition acceptable to God." You can only reach this condition through faith in Jesus Christ. In exchange for your faith, God counts you as righteous (i.e., being acceptable in his sight: Philippians 3:8–9). The breastplate of righteousness is forged by a combination of this perfect righteousness God imparts to you and your obedience to his commands for living. Your obedience is essential because it proves that your heart is in agreement with God and that your faith is genuine.

How the Breastplate Works

Your faith is the power link that connects your breastplate with God's infinite power. By believing in Jesus, you receive all the power and benefits of being righteous in God's sight. If you don't believe that you have God's righteousness, then your breastplate will be ineffective.

Your sin has an associated "spiritual nakedness" with it that repels God from us. When Adam and Eve sinned, they lost their covering of purity and became spiritually and physically naked. Their sin made them aware of their nakedness and separated them from fellowship with God. For the wages of sin is death (Romans 6:23). Now God mercifully slaughtered an animal and made clothes of the skin to cover Adam and Eve (Genesis 3:21).

Have you experienced spiritual nakedness:
_____
_____
_____
_____

AUTHOR'S EXAMPLE: My acceptance of salvation through the blood of Jesus made me aware of my spiritual nakedness throughout my life. My sin was so great (but no matter great or small), it kept me from having a relationship with my heavenly Father.

God's actions foreshadowed the lasting sacrifice he would make by sending Jesus to die on the cross for mankind. The blood of Christ provides atonement for your sin and clothes you with a righteousness (symbolized by a breastplate) that covers your spiritual nakedness. You can now boldly approach God's throne without fear of punishment (Romans 5:1; Hebrews 4:16).

Another important function of the breastplate of righteousness is revealed by the action of Christ's blood on your conscience. The blood of Jesus spiritually washes you clean from your sin (Hebrews 9:14, 10:22). This cleansing action removes the potential "footholds" that would have caused you to be vulnerable to the devil's attacks. With the breastplate of righteousness covering you through Christ's blood, the devil has nothing in you to exploit (John 14:30).

How to Put on the Breastplate

You put the breastplate on through faith by speaking it. Here is a way to do this:

"I put on the breastplate of righteousness. I believe in Jesus Christ as my Lord and Savior. I am clothed with God's righteousness, which protects my heart from the enemy. All footholds that the devil had in me have been washed away by the blood of Jesus. I am no longer clothed with filthy garments, but rather with rich robes of righteousness (Zechariah 3). The righteousness of God covers me and protects me from the enemy."

How to Maintain the Breastplate

Just as with conventional weapons of war, regular maintenance of your spiritual armor is critical to its operation in battle.

1. **Obey God's commands for living:** You are obligated to obey God's commands, out of loving appreciation for what Jesus did for you. This is a way of exercising your faith that keeps you plugged into God's power supply. Paul wrote, "Just as you used to offer the parts of your body in slavery to impurity and to ever-increasing wickedness, so now offer them in slavery to righteousness leading to holiness" (Romans 6:19). God gives you power to live obediently through the Holy Spirit (Romans 8:11, 13).

2. **Live in love:** Love is the key activity by which you live for righteousness. Jesus explained that all of the commandments are summed up by "love your neighbor as yourself" (Galatians 5:14). Paul wrote, "Therefore, as God's

chosen people, holy and dearly loved, clothe yourselves with compassion, kindness, humility, gentleness and patience. Bear with each other and forgive whatever grievances you may have against one another. Forgive as the Lord forgave you. And over all these virtues put on love, which binds them all together in perfect unity" (Colossians 3:12–14). By showing God's love to others, you will grow in righteousness toward holiness. When you combine your faith with living in love, your breastplate is strong, like an alloy of two metals.

Benefits of Living for Righteousness

A great benefit of living for righteousness is that your breastplate will function at maximum efficiency. Here are some other benefits that you will also enjoy:

1. **Protection:** "The righteousness of the upright will deliver them, but the unfaithful will be caught by their lust" (Proverbs 11:6).

2. **Prosperity and honor:** "He who pursues righteousness and love finds life, prosperity, and honor" (Proverbs 21:21).

3. **Filling with God's Spirit:** "Blessed are those who hunger and thirst for righteousness, for they will be filled" (Matthew 5:6).

4. **Quietness and confidence forever:** "The fruit of righteousness will be peace; the effect of righteousness will be quietness and confidence forever" (Isaiah 32:17).

5. **Reflection of God:** "You were taught, with regard to your former way of life, to put off your old self, which is being

corrupted by its deceitful desires; to be made new in the attitude of your mind; and to put on the new self, created to be like God in true righteousness and holiness" (Ephesians 4:22–24).

Thank you for showing me the truth about myself: that on my own, I could never be good enough to live in your presence. Thank you for taking my sins to the cross and offering me your righteous life. Lord, show me any sin that I need to confess right now, so that nothing will hinder me from being filled to overflowing with your Spirit. (Take a silent moment for your confession.) Thank you for forgiving me and for filling me with your righteous life.

"On my chest I put the breastplate of righteousness. I can fight any battle today because of the righteousness of Jesus, not my own! Jesus I declare that you are my righteousness and that through the victory of the cross I can stand victorious against temptation, sin and the attacks of our enemy" (2 Corinthians 5:12).

In the Old Testament, what group of people wore righteousness like a body armor?

_____
_____
_____
_____

What was this righteousness that they wore?

_____
_____
_____
_____

DANIEL BOEHM

Was this a good armor?_____Why?_____
_____
_____
_____
_____

Helmet of Salvation

"Take the helmet of salvation and the sword of the Spirit, which is the word of God" (Ephesians 6:17).

Helmet of Salvation: For protection of your mind and thinking against the lies of the wicked one. So that all your responses today, no matter what the circumstances (through words or actions), be according to the Father's will.

What are some lies that he has told you that have caused you to respond in a way that is unlike you?

_____
_____
_____

AUTHOR'S EXAMPLE: That I am right and that is all that matters, and because of that, I have taken my anger out on someone else who was innocent, or at least undeserving of my actions (e.g., getting angry with my wife for something she didn't do). He will use perception as a weapon against us because of what we perceive we believe, whether it is wrong or right.

The helmet was essential for the survival of a soldier in battle. Using the word "salvation" indicates that the helmet is a source of total deliverance. In Jesus, you can find deliverance in every situation: spiritual, emotional, and physical. He has to be your source, your guide, and your way out. You cannot deliver yourself.

Know the truth about God.

Embrace the Christian paradigm that says God promises daily and eternal salvation through Jesus Christ today (each day: Psalms 16 and 23; Hebrews 1:3–6) and forever (eternity: 2 Corinthians 4:16–18; 1 Thessalonians 4:17; and 1 John 3:13).

Beware of, recognize, and resist the world paradigm that teaches evolving spiritually by growing in consciousness and staying tuned to the cosmic mind.

Helmet: As defensive headgear worn by soldiers (1 Samuel 17:5–38; 2 Chronicles 26:14; Jeremiah 46:4; and Ezekiel 23:24).

Figurative: Isaiah 59:17, Ephesians 6:17, 1 Thessalonians 5:8

What is the significance of the helmet of salvation?

My acceptance of Jesus as Lord and Savior saves me (John 3:16). Thank Jesus for saving you and reclaim his protection, healing, and power for today and for eternity. Have you accepted Jesus? Put on the mind of Christ. One of the ways Satan pulls us down is through our mind: "As a man thinketh in his heart, so he is" (Proverbs 23:7). (What a person perceives, they believe.)

What does your heart say to you; what does it say that you are?
_____
_____
_____
_____

AUTHOR'S EXAMPLE: At one time, my heart listened to the enemy and had me convinced I wasn't worth living. Fortunately, God knew differently and intervened in my self-destructive plan. Now that I have received salvation through the blood of Christ Jesus, I know that I am a child of God and my life has value to him, me, and others.

Examine what you say to yourself or about yourself, what you think about, and how you think about others, and invite Jesus to replace your thoughts with his thoughts. The Bible says that you can "have the mind of Christ" (1 Corinthians 2:16b). Pray that "your attitude should be the same as that of Christ Jesus" (Philippians 2:5). Envision a helmet placed over your head to cleanse and protect your thoughts.

How will this help you tomorrow and all subsequent days?
_____
_____
_____
_____

"And he saw that there was no man, and wondered that there was no intercessor: therefore his arm brought salvation unto him; and his righteousness, it sustained him. For he put on righteousness as a breastplate, and a helmet of salvation upon his head" (Isaiah 59:16–17 KJV).

"But since we are of the day, let us be sober, having put on the breastplate of faith and love; and as a helmet, the hope of *salvation*" (1 Thessalonians 5:8 NAS).

"O God the Lord, the strength of my salvation, You have covered my head in the day of battle" (Psalm 140:7 NAS).

"And He is the head of the body, the church" (Colossians 1:18 NKJ).

"For who has known the mind of the Lord that he may instruct him? But we have *the mind of Christ*" (1 Corinthians 2:16 NIV).

"Let this *mind* be in you which was also in Christ Jesus" (Philippians 2:5 NKJ).

"Therefore, since Christ suffered for us in the flesh, arm yourselves also with the *same mind,* for he who has suffered in the flesh has ceased from sin" (1 Peter 4:1 NKJ).

"Indeed, we live as human beings, but we do not wage war according to human standards; for the weapons of our warfare are not merely human, but they have divine power to destroy strongholds. We destroy *arguments* and every proud obstacle raised up against the *knowledge of God,* and we take *every thought captive* to obey Christ" (2 Corinthians 10:3–5 NRS).

"We should no longer be children, tossed to and fro and carried about with every wind of doctrine, by the trickery of men, in the cunning craftiness of deceitful plotting, but, speaking the truth in love, may grow up in all things into Him who is the head—Christ—from whom the whole body, joined and knit together by what every joint supplies, according to the effective working by which every part does its share, causes growth of the body for the edifying of itself in love" (Ephesians 4:14–16 NKJ).

What is being said here about growing up?

_____
_____
_____
_____

AUTHOR'S EXAMPLE: Although the Bible tells us to come to God as little children, I believe this was done when we accepted Christ as our Lord and Savior. Now as Christian, we should have grown up through study of God's words and the use of his gifts. As such, we should no longer be blown about by winds of doctrine, nor believe in the lies that spew from the deceitfulness mouths of others. What better way for the boy to grow into a man than by becoming a warrior for Christ, thereby edifying himself through the righteousness of God?

The Importance of the Mind

Since humanity's beginning, Satan has focused his attacks on people's minds. Satan cannot force you to sin, but rather, he must persuade you to commit sin. The mind is the control center; it decides if you will sin or not. If you sin, you place yourself under the power of sin and become a slave to it (the degree will vary). Jesus said, "I tell you the truth, everyone who sins is a slave to sin" (John 8:34). If you choose to live as a slave to sin, you are mastered not only by your evil desires (Titus 3:3), but also by the devil, who temporarily rules the world (1 John 5:19). The devil seeks to persuade you to sin because it will increase his own power and influence in the world.

It is time to break your bondage from sin, tear off the shackles of regret, straighten your back of resistance, and stand for truth in the word of God.

Jesus authors your faith, and while you learn about the truth through study of the Bible, you are filling and strengthening your mind against the wiles of Satan. You must not only learn, you must put into action what you have learned. Faith based on God's word is the most powerful kind of faith. Jesus said, "I tell you the truth, if you have faith as small as a mustard seed, you can say to this mountain, 'move from here to there' and it will move. Nothing will be impossible for you" (Matthew 17:20). When your shield of faith is rooted in this kind of faith, the devil cannot penetrate your defenses because all of his "flaming arrows" are quenched by the shield (Ephesians 6:16). However, if Satan can corrupt your faith, bringing it away from God's word by tainting it with doubt, your shield will be compromised. Therefore, you must wear our helmet to protect your mind, where your faith is held strongly in defense against Satan's attempts at corruption.

You should be aware that the power of faith can be used for sinful purposes, and Satan seeks to harness that power. Jesus' statement in Matthew 17:20 guaranteed that power of faith, regardless of the bearer's intentions. Satan therefore wants to persuade you to misuse your faith to further his purposes.

How can faith be used for a sinful purpose?
_____
_____
_____

AUTHOR'S EXAMPLE: By allowing myself to believe in my own good works, I believed (had faith) that I was going to heaven when I died. This made Satan very happy because his work was done, since we all know that sin is death, and my sin was great. I was destined for an eternity in hell.

Satan's Tactics against the Mind

Satan uses a variety of tactics against your mind. These are designed to weaken your faith, ruin your discernment, and corrupt your thoughts. If successful, these "spiritual head wounds" will make it easier for Satan to captivate your mind to do his will (2 Timothy 2:26). Here are some examples of typical tactics Satan uses against your mind:

1. **Deceive with false doctrine:** False doctrine leads people astray from their devotion to Christ. For example, Paul was worried that false teachers may have led the Corinthians astray from their devotion to Christ (2 Corinthians 11:3). False doctrine ultimately brings you into bondage under lies. Examples:

    - smooth talk and flattery to deceive minds (Romans 16:18)

- deceitful scheming through the cunning and craftiness (Ephesians 4:14)
- trivial doctrinal disputes (2 Peter 1:16; 1 Timothy 1:3–7, 4:7–8)
- demons teaching false doctrines (1 Timothy 4:1–2)

2. **Distract with carnal interests:** Satan tempted Eve by appealing to her carnal interests (Genesis 3:4–6), and he continues to tempt people today through combinations of pride, lust of the eyes, and lust of the flesh (1 John 2:15–17). The more you yield to the temptations, the more your mind becomes set on earthly things instead of godly things.

An earthly mind-set weakens your devotion to God and causes you to be unfruitful for God's kingdom. It could even cause you to become hostile toward God. Paul wrote, "Those who live according to the sinful nature have their minds set on what that nature desires; but those who live in accordance with the Spirit have their minds set on what the Spirit desires. The mind of sinful man is death, but the mind controlled by the Spirit is life and peace; the sinful mind is hostile to God. It does not submit to God's law, nor can it do so" (Romans 8:5–7). Here are some examples of carnal distractions:

- pride (Matthew 16:23; Luke 4:3–13)
- cares of the world (Philippians 3:19; Colossians 3:1–2; Matthew 13:22)
- money (Matthew 13:22; 1 Timothy 6:5, 10; John 12:2–8; Acts 5:1–11)
- sexual temptations (Proverbs 6:23–29, 7:6–27; 1 Corinthians 5, 6:12–20; Revelation 2:20–23; 2 Timothy 2:22)

3. **Poison the mind or blind to the truth:** Well-timed or well-placed lies can quickly find a home in your mind if you are not firmly rooted in the truth. You are especially vulnerable when you have issues like unforgiveness and roots of rejection. If you believe what the devil says to you, you are in danger of a partial or total blinding of the truth. As with the false doctrine tactic, believing such lies places you in bondage because you are unable to receive the truth that would set you free (John 8:31–32). Here are some examples:

   - poison the mind against other Christians (Acts 14:2)
   - blind the minds of non-Christians to the truth (2 Corinthians 4:4)
   - corrupt the mind and conscience (Titus 1:15)
   - sear the conscience via false doctrines (1 Timothy 4:2)

The long-term effects of these untreated "spiritual head wounds" can be devastating. Paul described a group of people in Romans 1:18–32 who turned completely away from God. They followed a path of increasing rebellion, resulting in total abandonment to evil. Key changes occurred in their minds along the way. Their thinking became "futile," and their "foolish hearts were darkened" (21). They exchanged the truth of God for a lie (25) and committed sexual sin. Eventually, God gave them over to a "depraved mind" (28), and they were filled with every form of evil (29–31). (Another example is Ephesians 4:17–19.)

How the Helmet of Salvation Protects Your Mind

Considering the strategic value of our minds, God has given you the helmet of salvation to protect us from the enemy. This helmet functions by the peace of God, which is engaged when your mind is focused on God and trusting in him. Consider these verses that link God's peace to your mind:

"Do not be anxious about anything, but in everything, by prayer and petition, with thanksgiving, present your requests to God. And the peace of God, which transcends all understanding, will guard your hearts and your minds in Christ Jesus" (Philippians 4:6-7). "You will keep him in perfect peace him whose mind is steadfast, because he trusts in you" (Isaiah 26:3).

The helmet, like the other pieces of armor, is dependent on your faith in God and his promises.

How to Put the Helmet On

- Speak it on by faith, believing that you truly have the mind of Christ (1 Corinthians 2:16). You can stand on God's promise that he has written his laws on your mind. Hebrews 10:16 says, "This is the covenant I will make with them after that time, says the Lord. I will put my laws in their hearts, and I will write them on their minds." This can be as simple as saying: "I put on the helmet of salvation, which protects my mind from the enemy's attacks. I have the mind of Christ."

- Focus your thoughts on God instead of sinful things: Paul wrote in Colossians 3:2, "Set your minds on the things above, not on earthly things." This discipline will likely be the most challenging part of walking in purity. The more you do it, the easier it will become. It basically involves redirecting your thoughts toward God or godly things whenever you are being tempted. In my own practice of this, I have found that speaking Bible verses, singing praise and worship songs, picturing Jesus on the cross, and saying, "The blood of Jesus covers me," are all helpful in shifting my thoughts heavenward.

As you practice this "thought shifting," the Holy Spirit will help you improve your recognition of the times when your thoughts are going awry. It's important that you take action at the moment of recognition to redirect your thoughts heavenward. Any delay could lead to sin.

Your obedience in controlling your thoughts will reflect your love for God. In doing so, you will fulfill Jesus' command in Matthew 22:37 to "love the Lord your God with all your heart and with all your soul and with all your mind."

- Direct your requests to God through prayer: Situations will come your way that will tempt you to get anxious and take matters into your own hands instead of taking them to God. By taking your requests to God, you enable God's perfect peace to protect your mind and heart (Philippians 4:6-7). Your prayers should always include thanking God for who he is and what he has done in your life.

"O God the Lord, the strength of my salvation, You have covered my head in the day of battle" (Psalm 140:7).

Thank you for promising me salvation both for today's battles and for all eternity. On my head, I receive the helmet of salvation. Jesus, you are my salvation. You are my deliverance. Deliver me from all sins and weaknesses: spiritual, physical, and emotional. Cover me with strength, peace and anointing and bring me to complete wholeness in you (1 Thessalonians 5:8-9).

The helmet, like the breastplate, protects vital organs, only in this case, the head holds all the controlling functions of the body, and if damaged, the remainder of the body no longer functions. But because of the blood of Jesus, you are now saved, as before you were damned. The helmet of salvation protects you from spiritual blows. A physical blow to the head would have ended your life and sent you plummeting into everlasting damnation. Whereby with the spiritual helmet, even if your physical body is destroyed, your life continues anew in an everlasting life of joy and peace. So as the physical helmet protects your mind, the spiritual helmet protects your thoughts, and through this protects your spirit.

How do you relate the helmet to salvation?
_____
_____
_____
_____

Do you see the benefit of putting it on every day?
_____
_____
_____
_____

Shield of Faith

"Above all, taking the shield of faith with which you will be able to quench all the fiery darts of the wicked one" (Ephesians 6:16).

Shield of Faith: It is able to quench the fiery darts of the wicked one, allowing you to walk in faith, trusting in the Lord and not yourself.

The only protection against the archers' arrows that rained down from the battlements in ancient warfare was the shield. Shields were primarily used as individual protection, if used correctly; it was a trustworthy piece of equipment that could be used individually or joined with others to create a large wall of protection. If dropped, it became useless, and the soldier's fate rested in his skill with weapons.

AUTHOR'S EXAMPLE: As the Romans were attacking a walled city, archers along the walls would rain down arrows. The Roman soldiers with overlapping shields could continue advancing toward the gates of the city despite the arrows, for their shield became a large wall of protection.

You trust in Jesus alone as your shield, for you cannot rely on your own abilities in this battle. For without the shield of faith, you would be like a Roman soldier who dropped his shield in the midst of battle: defenseless.

Think of an example you can share where you put your faith in yourself rather than Jesus, and share what the outcome of this was.

_____
_____
_____
_____

AUTHOR'S EXAMPLE: There was a time in my life when I was young and very angry, and I pitted my driving skills against a mountain road. Fortunately, before I killed myself or someone else, the right rear tire on my car blew out. Now I had a spare and a jack, but I did not have a tire iron, so I spent a long quiet night in the mountains with more than enough time to cool off. It was during this time that I realize that my driving skills would not be up to the challenge of the next set of curves. I believe that if I had looked hard enough, I would have seen the hand of God choosing the location and the cause that took out my tire and saved my life. This was misplaced faith, for if I had placed my faith in Jesus, I would have never allowed my anger to get that far out of control.

Know the truth about God.

Embrace the Christian paradigm that says to live in faith through our continual trust in God, his word, and his promises (Romans 4:18–21; Hebrews 11:1; and 1 Peter 1:6–7).

Beware of, recognize, and resist the world paradigm that teaches to trust in self, inner wisdom, dreams, visions, gods, goddess, cosmic forces, and coincidences.

What are some things in which you may have placed or had misdirected faith in?

_____
_____
_____
_____

AUTHOR'S EXAMPLE: (In the early 1980's I was part of the Cody Country Gunfighters, a group of people who put on gunfights for the tourist trade in Cody Wyoming. I did this for three years). At one point in my gun-fighting career, we all placed our faith in the belief that the person who was loading the blanks was doing it right and that the other actors were as conscientious as I was. The results was my brother lost the cornea off his left eye, rendering him legally blind, and I was knocked unconscious in a gunfight from the percussion of being shot in the back of the head. This resulted in a hospital trip and the loss of my equilibrium for a period of time.

Can you use some of the world paradigms to strengthen your faith and belief?

_____

_____

_____

_____

AUTHOR'S EXAMPLE: My answer would have to be yes: I believe that trust in self and inner wisdom is required if you believe that the Holy Spirit is leading you; this can be tested according to biblical standards.

I believe that God gives us dreams and that without dreams, we are not truly living according to God's will. God gives us dreams to help others, to grow in Spirit, and yes even to become financially successful (remember: He who God has given a lot, a lot is expected of him). I believe the world paradigm dream is actually fantasy, and there is a huge difference between dreams and fantasies. If a dream is only self-serving, then is it not a fantasy or the start of a potential nightmare?

I believe in visions and vision casting, because if you are blessed with the ability to see what could be, you could identify the methods to teach others how to achieve better lives through godly means (by serving others, following unctions that are inspired by the Holy Spirit, and living a Christian life).

I believe in only one God and no goddesses. Cosmic forces are out there, and coincidences do happen, but these are not things you put faith in for your salvation.

The shield is a defensive armor, the chief means of personal protection. It is carried in one hand or on the arm to ward off

enemy blows, freeing the other hand to use weapons of offense. There were many different kinds of shields; some were called bucklers, and others were targets (Psalm 35:2 and Ezekiel 38:4).

Figuratively, the shield of faith signifies the protection of God (Genesis 15:1 and Psalm 5:12), God's truth (Psalm 91:4), or an entire army (Jeremiah 46:3).

"Take the great shield of faith, on which you will be able to quench all the flaming darts of the Wicked one" (Ephesians 6:16 Wey).

What are the fiery darts that the spiritual shield protects you from?

_____
_____
_____
_____

The arrows with which you are assaulted are temptations, fears, and doubts about God and yourself. The shield Paul writes about is large and thick. When burning arrows were shot in warfare, the arrows sunk into the thick, layered wood of the shield and were quickly extinguished. Envision yourself holding a large shield with which you can stop any burning arrow shot at you. This shield is faith in Christ Jesus, who let Satan do his worst to him in the desert, who died on the cross, and who rose up in victory. "Thanks be to God who gives us the victory through our Lord Jesus Christ" (1 Corinthians 15:57).

"Contend, O Lord, with those who contend with me; fight against those who fight against me. Take up shield and buckler; arise and come to my aid. Brandish spear and javelin against those who pursue me. Say to my soul, 'I am your salvation.' ... Then my soul will rejoice in the Lord and delight in his salvation" (Psalm 35:1–3, 9 NIV).

"Many are saying of my soul, There is no salvation for him in God. Selah. But You, O Jehovah, are a shield around me; You are my glory and He who lifts up my head" (Psalm 3:2–3 GLT).

"We wait in hope for the Lord; he is our help and our shield" (Psalm 33:20 NIV).

"Fight the good fight of the faith. Take hold of the eternal life to which you were called when you made your good confession in the presence of many witnesses" (1 Timothy 6:12 NIV).

What is the good confession being talked about here?
_____
_____
_____
_____

"For every child of God overcomes the world; and the victorious principle which has overcome the world is our *faith*. Who but the man that believes that Jesus is the Son of God overcomes the world?" (1 John 5:4–5 Wey).

"Every word of God is flawless; he is a shield to those who take refuge in him" (Proverbs 30:5 NIV)

"Who are *protected* by the power of God through faith for a salvation ready to be revealed in the last time" (1 Peter 1:5 NAS).

To best understand what "faith" means, let's consider these definitions:

1. The Greek word for "faith" in the above verses is *pistis*, which means "conviction of the truth of anything, belief in the conviction or respecting man's relationship to God and divine things, generally with the included idea of trust and holy fervor born of faith and joined with it."

ARMOR OF GOD

2. Hebrews 11:1 provides further insight on the meaning of faith: "Now faith is the substance of things hoped for, the evidence of things not seen."

Putting these definitions together in practical terms, faith in God is
- trusting in God's word as truth,
- trusting that God will provide for your needs,
- trusting that God will protect you from the evil one,
- believing that God is with you and lives in you, even though you may not see him,
- believing that Christ's sacrifice paid the penalty for your sin, reconciling you to God, and
- believing that through faith you have Christ's authority over evil powers.

In your human weakness, you may find it difficult to fully trust and believe God in the above ways. Since God is the author, "perfecter," and finisher of your faith (Hebrews 12:2), you can and should ask him for the completion of your faith. For example, Jesus told the man whose son had an evil spirit, "Everything is possible for him who believes" (Mark 9:23–25).

Just as the Father asked Jesus for help in overcoming unbelief, you too can ask Jesus to help you overcome your doubt. As a result, your shield of faith will operate at its maximum strength.

Where do you find doubt strongest in your walk?

_____
_____
_____
_____

AUTHOR'S EXAMPLE: For me, it is when I think I have tried everything possible and still things haven't changed, and I let doubt seep into my heart, my mind, and sometimes even my soul. At these times, I feel hopelessness settling into my very bones and feel like giving up. Then I realize it is not giving up that is required but giving in and giving over to God that which I can't deal with on my own. That is when I realize my faith is being tested, and I must choose to stop trying to rely on myself and start placing my faith in God.

When we believe in something, our belief gives it power to manifest in our lives. Jesus said, "Everything is possible for him who believes" (Mark 9:23).

Do you believe that? _____ Why or why not? _____
_____
_____
_____
_____

We must take care that we believe God's word and not Satan's lies. If we believe the enemies lies, we're putting faith into them and opening a door for the enemy to influence us. This is "negative faith," and the irony of it is, that we give it power, through our own belief in the lies.

What in your life could be an example of this? ____
_____
_____
_____
_____

AUTHOR'S EXAMPLE: I used to believe I was going to heaven because I wasn't that bad. The enemy had me convinced through my belief in his deceits that I was saved through my works rather than the blood of Jesus.

Your faith must be based on the truth of the word of God. Any other source is neither reliable nor trustworthy. Satan's primary tactic against your faith is to persuade you to believe lies, so that your faith is not founded on truth. Once you believe lies, your shield of faith is hanging limp by your side or lying on the ground at your feet, doing little if any good for self-defense.

Which lies are more damaging: the ones you tell yourself or the ones you tell others so often you then believe them to be truths?

___

AUTHOR'S EXAMPLE: Self-lie is when you tell yourself, "It's okay if I do it this time; it is only once"; this then makes it easier to do it again the next time. Others may start out as a small lie but they take another lie to cover it and another to cover that one, until what started as a small deceit often turns into a big lie. Each time you give in to sin, the shield weakens, and you become more open to further attacks by the enemy.

Satan often entices people into sexual sin with the lie that God's plan for sex isn't sufficient or isn't worth the wait for marriage. He offers attractive counterfeits through prostitution, pornography, homosexuality, chat rooms, phone sex, fornication, and masturbation, in an attempt to persuade us to make our own sexual provision instead of trusting God for it. This shift of faith away from God weakens your shield of faith. As a result, you open yourself up for further deception and destruction from the enemy.

What lies did you believe about sexual sin?

___

AUTHOR'S EXAMPLE: At one time, I believed that prostitution was a good thing, because if you did it with a prostitute, it wasn't really cheating; it was a business transaction. I actually thought you could use a whorehouse to make money and use it to help others, and this too would make it a good thing.

Temptation seeks to inflame your sinful desires (e.g., lust of the flesh, lust of the eyes, pride of life, etc.) by stirring up your thoughts of fulfilling those desires. If your faith is operating effectively, the enemy's temptations will not be able to inflame sinful desires in you, because you won't believe the lies behind them.

How has temptation influenced your actions?
___
___
___
___

AUTHOR'S EXAMPLE: One of Satan's favorite pathways into my life was through excessive self-pride; it made me think that I was better than others (e.g., in better physical shape, financially secure, thinking I could do most things better than others). The easiest pathway was through my eye gate by way of pornography, sexual enticement, or selfish desires.

The proper use of your shield of faith hinges upon the principle that you believe God's truth, thereby speaking what you believe (2 Corinthians 4:13–14). Your spoken words of faith set the shield into place on your arm, facing the enemy's darts with confidence and faith. The spoken words of faith would also allow the shield to become an offensive weapon as well as a defensive one. With faith, belief in the unseen truth in the word of God, your shield is up and covering you and leading you into battle.

What is the size of your shield of faith? Do you have shields of differing sizes?
___
___
___
___

AUTHOR'S EXAMPLE: In my daily walk, I am attacked by varying degrees of fiery darts through temptations of the eyes, mind, and the personal weakness in my own belief of whose I am. For different temptations, it takes different sized shields; one may be small and a matter of choice, or they may be larger, requiring asking God for help through the Holy Spirit. Then there are the times where I must call upon the almighty word of God and verbally command the evil one to depart from my thoughts, turning these thoughts to the things of God and his majestic creation.

Then there are times when I don't realize it but I am using a smaller shield, and the forsaken one inches into my thoughts, tempting me to do something that I should not—or even think of things that I should not. For the Bible says that thinking some things is the same as doing them, for your mind has already committed the sin. So where is the battle ground? The battle ground is in the mind. Realize that there are many types and sizes of shields, so don't let your guard (your spiritual shield) down; keep them with you and always hold them firmly before you and walk in the light of the Lord.

Finally, ask God to strengthen and perfect your faith in any area that it is weak by reaffirming your faith through daily intake of God's word. You will then be able to use it to destroy the incoming lies behind the temptations you face on a daily basis, as you extend the shield of faith over yourself and your family.

Oh Lord, thank you for helping me to have faith in you. I choose to count on everything you have shown me about yourself and everything you have promised me in your word. In my hand, I take up the shield of faith. Father, by faith, connect me to the power of Jesus. My desire is to trust in you and your strength alone. Protect me from the arrows of the enemy today as I rely on your power. Give me faith so I may go forward doing your will (Hebrews 11:33–34).

What is faith, and how is it described?
_____
_____
_____
_____

(Dictionary: to trust, confide in, unquestioning belief in God, religion, etc.)

DANIEL BOEHM

What are some of the things you have faith in and why?

_____
_____
_____

Do religions have their belief (faith) grounded in truth?

_____

Which ones?

_____

How

_____

How would you relate faith to a shield?

_____
_____
_____

AUTHOR'S EXAMPLE: I believed in the self-doubts others cast upon me, and as I grew older and stronger in my faith, small things no longer bothered me. Then as I grew in my strength in Christ, I no longer believed in the lies. I no longer doubted in my salvation; my faith backed by knowledge is now unshakable.

Sword of the Spirit

Speak His Word with Strength and Accuracy
The Sword is the Word of God. Read It. Study It. Know It

The sword of the spirit is a powerful weapon of spiritual warfare. When you use the sword properly, God's power and resources are available to you. The sword relies on faith for its foundation. When your faith is based on the promises of God's word, it engages your sword's spiritual power link to God., "If you can believe", Jesus said "all things are possible to him who believes." (Mark 9:23 NIV). Spoken in faith, the sword of the spirit is the truth that sets people free from the lies that hold them captive.

Know the truth about God.

Embrace the Christian paradigm that says to use the power of God's word to counter deception and accusation and to triumph over spiritual foes (Hebrews 4:12; Matthew 4:2–11; 1 Peter 3:15; and Psalm 119:110–112).

Beware of, recognize, and resist the world paradigm that teaches the power of thoughts, words, and affirmations to change reality to direct spiritual forces.

Literally: A sword is a sharp-edged metal weapon of varying styles, which include double edged, single edged, and varied lengths; each requires certain skills for its use. When used by soldiers in hand-to-hand combat, they deliver cutting or stabbing blows to the enemy (Jeremiah 46:3–4 and Ephesians 6:14–17).

Figuratively: Romans 13:12; 2 Corinthians 6:7, 10:4; Ephesians 6:11–17; and 1 Thessalonians 5:8.

When used at close range by a skilled soldier, the sword is a deadly weapon. Paul tells us that the sword represents the word of God, the written picture of Jesus. He is the living version of everything God wanted to say to mankind. God's word is a powerful weapon against our enemy when it's used under the spirit's power and direction.

The metaphorical sword of the spirit signifies the word of God that you speak with strength and accuracy. The sword is the word of God; read it, study it, and know it. Claim its power, read and study your Bible, and memorize sections of it so that you have God's word on your heart and are ready when you are tested. Listen also for God's living word in every event or inner nudging of your day or night.

AUTHOR'S EXAMPLE: There are times when I get an unction, a feeling that I should say or do something, but I don't really know why. However, I have found that when I listen and do what I am told, something good usually comes from it.

"God works together with those who love Him to make GOOD in ALL THINGS" (Romans 8:28). But the fruit of the spirit is love, joy, peace, longsuffering, gentleness, goodness, faith, meekness, and temperance.

So often you get tied in knots: family or cultural traditions, habits or addictions, promises you have made, or rules that others (not God) have written on your heart. Fears, desires, and all kinds of spiritual forces of and in your world hold you in bondage. As you see these threats, temptations, illnesses, and habits that prevent you from living in health and freedom, visualize Jesus giving you the sword of the spirit. Take it and sever any bonds that have imprisoned you.

Is the sword of the spirit one sword or many?

___

___

___

Did Paul intend for Christians to have only one sword to take into battle? The common understanding, that the sword of the spirit is "the entire Bible itself as one big sword," is limited and weakens a Christian's ability to fight effectively in spiritual warfare. Read it again; Paul is saying much more in this verse. Just as historical functional swords were designed for specific fighting styles, each Bible verse can be very powerful, depending upon the situation. Historical swords varied greatly in their size, design, and the techniques required to master their use. Pick the right verse for the right temptation (i.e., the best sword of the spirit [scripture] for the battle at hand). The key point in spiritual warfare is for Christians to memorize key verses in the Bible so you can have them ready for immediate use when your mind and thoughts are under attack.

Jesus used the sword of the spirit in resisting Satan in the wilderness (Matthew 4:1–11). Jesus responded to each of the temptations by quoting specific scripture. The scripture he chose revealed and destroyed the lies of each temptation. In the same way, you can use scripture to destroy the lies that tempt you. Of course, the spiritual attacks did not come when Jesus was at his physical best; rather, it was at the beginning of his ministry and after being in the wilderness, fasting for forty days.

When are you at your weakest spiritually?

_____
_____
_____

AUTHOR'S EXAMPLE: If you are given additional change, do you keep it? You see a lovely young lady dressed in a provocative manner; how far does your mind take you down the wrong path? You tell a white lie; does it stop there? You pick up a magazine, and your eyes linger on the model standing next to the car, bike, or boat; how long does your focus linger?

Remember: Even Satan used scripture to justify the temptation (Psalm 91:11–12).

"He has made My mouth like a sharp sword, In the shadow of His hand He has concealed Me; And He has also made Me a select arrow, He has hidden Me in His quiver" (Isaiah 49:2 NAS).

"For the word of God is living and powerful, and sharper than any two-edged sword, piercing even to the division of soul and spirit, and of joints and marrow, and is a discerner of the thoughts and intents of the heart. And there is no creature hidden from His sight, but all things are naked and open to the eyes of Him to whom we must give account" (Hebrews 4:12–13 NKJ).

Also remember that even your thoughts are an open book to Him, so no matter what you do, the Creator already knows.

"In truthful speech and in the power of God; with weapons of righteousness in the right hand and in the left" (2 Corinthians 6:7 NIV).

"For the Lord takes delight in his people; he crowns the humble with salvation. Let the saints rejoice in this honor and sing for joy on their beds. May the praise of God be in their mouths and a double-edged sword in their hands" (Psalm 149:4–6 NIV).

"To the Christian armed for defense in battle, the apostle recommends only one weapon of attack; but it is enough, the sword of the Spirit, which is the word of God. It subdues and mortifies evil desires and blasphemous thoughts as they rise within; and answers unbelief and error as they assault from without. A single text, well understood, and rightly applied, at once destroys a temptation or an objection, and subdues the most formidable adversary" (Matthew Henry).

Know that on the average, people are easily driven by temptation toward immediate gratification, and there is no lasting peace or joy in your life unless you find it through God.

When was the last time you succumbed to immediate gratification?

_____
_____
_____
_____

What was it that you succumbed to and why?

_____
_____
_____
_____

Satan does not want you to glorify God with praise and worship. A secondary strategy to fight temptation would also include praising God. Simply start listing in your mind everything you are thankful for (God's blessings, forgiveness, etc.). When you feel tempted, focus your thoughts on praising God. Use them to replace thoughts based in temptation.

From the very beginning, God has spoken words that have powerfully influenced everything that exists. For example, God created the heavens and earth by speaking them into existence. The Bible says that by faith we understand that the world was prepared by the word of God, so that what is seen was not made out of things which are visible. Since God created you in his likeness, you too have the ability to release power through speech.

For example, your words can bring life and death (Proverbs 18:21). They can build people up or tear them down (James 3):

- A group of believers prayed the word, and the result was that the place was shaken; they were all filled with the Holy Spirit and spoke the word of God boldly (Acts 4:24-31).
- Preaching the word (Acts 13:38-43).
- Answering questions with the word (Acts 13:46-68).
- Singing the word (Acts 16:25-34).

Basic Training: When using the sword of the spirit, we need to ensure that we are using the scripture in the proper context. In order to understand the context, we'll need to learn the Bible. Bible study not only familiarizes us with the word, it also builds our faith up (Romans 10:17) and sharpens our discernment skills for spiritual warfare (Hebrews 4:12).

- **Have daily quiet times:** The best method for learning the Bible is to study it each day in a quiet time with God. Specifically, you'll want to learn about God's promises to you, your identity in Jesus Christ, and the guidelines for holy living.
- **Memorize key verses:** As you study the Bible, you'll also want to pick out verses to memorize. Scripture memory helps improve your swordsmanship in rejecting

temptations. It usually requires persistence and effort, but it is well worth it.
- **Practice:** As you face temptations each day, try to recall the verses you have learned that apply to the temptation. You can ask the Holy Spirit to help you remember them. One of the Holy Spirit's functions is to remind you of the word (John 14:26). The more you have memorized, the more verses the Spirit has to help you with! The more you speak the scriptures that come to mind, the more you reinforce them in your memory.

Each of us has our own weak areas of attack by temptation, but they are not necessarily the same for each person. Where some are very vulnerable, others are not as tempted. The areas you are tempted in can change minute by minute, and others remain the same throughout your life. The list of physical areas subject to attack is long, but the list of areas subject to temptation is even longer. You need to look within yourself to identify your own areas that have become targets for temptation and spiritual warfare. Therefore, you must find scriptures that specifically address this weakness and memorize them. The goal is to prepare your mind in advance with specific Bible verses, each serving as a sword of the spirit for each specific area of attack.

Just like in real swordplay, if you use the wrong sword at the wrong time or in the wrong conditions, your results might not be what you had in mind. Develop your collection of spiritual swords so you will be prepared in all circumstances. A great starting place is to memorize key scripture verses. If you don't know the Bible well enough to find them, start by memorizing the verses Jesus quoted above. Another option is to ask someone you know to be a Christian for help.

Thank you for the scriptures you have given me to memorize. Please show me which one(s) you want me to use to cut through deceptions and gain your victory in any battle I may face today.

If you don't have one, now is time to start looking for what I call a life verse, a verse that will dwell in your heart to guide you through life, and one that will encourage and empower you to do that for which God has chosen you. Whether it be for a season or a lifetime, let it become your driving force to become a follower and a warrior for Christ.

AUTHOR'S EXAMPLE: "The Lord is my shepherd, I lack nothing. He makes me lie down in green pastures, he leads me beside quiet waters, he refreshes my soul. He guides me along the right paths for his name's sake. Even though I walk through the darkest valley, I will fear no evil, for you are with me; your rod and your staff, they comfort me. You prepare a table before me in the presence of my enemies. You anoint my head with oil; my cup overflows. Surely your goodness and love will follow me all the days of my life, and I will dwell in the house of the Lord forever." (Psalm 23:1-6 NIV)

In my hand, I take up the sword of the spirit, the powerful word of God. Jesus, you are the living version of God's word. May God's word give me wisdom to apply the word to life's situations and today's troubles (Hebrews 4:12).

Is the word of God the only offensive weapon? Why or why not?

_____
_____
_____
_____

AUTHOR'S EXAMPLE: When spoken, even you can command the antagonist and send him away. You can parry, thrust, and counter attacks of the enemy by striking out, hunting down, and destroying evil wherever you may find it. You can move forward or stand and defend, step in between evil and the lost. The word of God stands true in all things.

Is there a secondary offensive weapon in your immediate arsenal?

_____
_____
_____
_____

AUTHOR'S EXAMPLE: The shield is commonly and primarily used in defense; however, it can be (and is) a formidable weapon in the right hands.

How will you prepare your arsenal?

_____
_____
_____
_____

Review

Sandals of Peace: Thank you for the peace you give me when I trust and follow you. Show me how to help others find that peace, for without You in my life, I could not have peace. The "peace that transcends all understanding" (Philippians 4:7) is available to me only as I give my life entirely over to your control. As I strap on my sandals each day, I give my cares and concerns to you and ask you to carry them. Your peace will be left in their place.

Belt of Truth: Thank you, my Lord, for showing me the truth about yourself. Thank you for reminding me that you are the only God, the Creator of heaven and earth, the King of the universe, my Father who loves me, and my Shepherd who leads me. You are my wisdom, my counselor, my hope, and my strength. You are everything I need each day, so I buckle it securely around my waist, knowing that you are with me every step of the way. You alone are the truth in life. I will spend time in your word and learn your truth.

Breastplate of Righteousness: Thank you for showing me the truth about myself: that on my own, I could never be good enough to live in your presence. Thank you for taking my sins to the cross and offering me your righteous life. Lord, show me any sin that I need to confess right now, so that nothing will hinder me from being filled to overflowing with your spirit. Thank you for forgiving me and for filling me with your righteous life as I put on your breastplate, and thank you for your never-ending mercy toward us. You have given us righteousness when we follow you. You will teach us every day if we open our eyes and ears to see and hear you. The cross is an excellent example of your mercy to us. You gave your Son for us so that we may spend eternity with you.

Helmet of Salvation: Thank you for promising me salvation both for today's battles and for all eternity. I know that I have been saved to battle together with you against evil here on the planet earth. I can do so willingly, knowing that I will spend eternity with you.

Shield of Faith: Thank you for helping me have faith in you. I choose to count on everything you have shown me about yourself and everything you have promised me in your word. This is another defensive weapon in my arsenal. I use this piece of armor to guard against the constant assaults by the enemy. Each morning as I pick up my shield, I thank you for my faith, faith that comes in knowing he will never leave or forsake me (Deuteronomy 31:8).

The Sword of the Spirit: Thank you for the scriptures you have given me to memorize. Please show me which one(s) you want me to use to cut through deceptions and gain your victory in any battle I may face this day. This is the only offensive weapon in the armor of God mentioned in this passage. My sword is your word, the Bible. With it, I can slay the evil in the world as it presents itself to me. I will read your Bible, learn your word, and memorize your verses. I will keep them on the tip of my tongue.

Dressed in this armor daily, you are prepared to enter the world. Without it, you will be prey to attack. Think about each piece as you put it on. Thank God for supplying you with his armor to protect you.

Now you must learn how to don the armor you have studied so that you can be prepared to stand and battle against the temptations and evil in the world. So as you enter in battle each day, don the wardrobe God has provided you to wear. As you dress in the morning, you need to suit up in God's armor as well. "Finally, be strong in the Lord and in his mighty power. I will put on the full armor of God so that I can take a stand against the devil's schemes. For our struggle is not against flesh and blood, but against the powers of the ruling authorities of this dark world and against the spiritual forces of evil in the heavenly realms. Therefore I put on the full armor of God, so that when the day of evil comes, I will be able to stand my ground, and after doing everything, to stand firm then, with my feet fitted with the readiness that comes from the gospel of peace, with the belt of truth buckled around my waist, with the breastplate of righteousness in place. In addition to all this, I take up the shield of faith, with which I can extinguish all the flaming arrows of the evil one. I place the helmet of salvation upon my head and pick up the sword of the Spirit, which is the word of God. I will pray in the Spirit on all occasions, all kinds of prayers and requests. I will keep this in mind, be alert and always keep on praying in Jesus awesome and powerful name" (Ephesians 6:10–18).

Father God, help me this day to prepare myself for the rigors of life that include putting my life on the line for your glory. Help me to properly don the sandals of peace, by lacing them tightly to my feet to keep my steps sure and sound, preventing me from the pitfalls of life that the enemy places before me. Help me to place the belt of truth securely around my waist so that I may be able to identify the truth from lies and grant me discernment to see with unveiled eyes the deceptions of the enemy, so that I may be prepared in all things. Lord, as I hold the breastplate to my body, let your spirit tighten the straps and secure the buckles to hold it in place, so that I may stand in your righteousness and mercy. As I place the helmet of salvation upon my head, may your word echo in my mind to remind me whose I am. When the enemy attempts to distract me, remind me that you are always there with me, to lead me in and through all things.

Abba Father, my body is now clothed in your armor, and I now stand armored against the wiles of the enemy, and before me stands the shield of faith. As I prepare to pick up my shield, I think of how God leads his chosen into battle against outstanding odds and know that he now leads me. With faith going before, defending me from the assault of the enemy in all his forms, I am protected against the evil of this world. Help me to go forth, always forward, advancing into the realm held by the adversary, who hides from you in deception and lies.

Lastly, before I pick up the sword of the spirit, I stand humbled before your throne and ask that you grant me all courage, wisdom, and strength, all of which is needed to wield your mighty sword, the word, and to strike out in your blessed and holy name. To meet the adversary head on and to challenge the wrong in this world, as I strive to stand in the gap before the adversary for myself and those who cannot stand for themselves.

So now I grasp the hilt and draw forth the sword of the spirit, feeling the balance shift in my hand as it fits itself to the present need. For both the sword of the spirit and the shield of faith are multifaceted and will change, as the situation requires.

Father, I now stand before you, fitted with the armor of God, and at this time, I am prepared as best as I may be. Battle ready and humbled in your presence, I bow my head and take to my knee as I offer my fealty and service with this, a soldier's prayer:

Lord God, Father, and King, I give of myself to you fully and completely, so that you may use me as you choose in this war with the enemy. I only ask you grant me wisdom, courage, strength, and discernment to follow where you will lead and do what it is you will have me do. Not to fold under pressure but to always move forward over, around, or through the obstacles placed before me by the enemy, all the while preparing the way so that others may follow.

Now I rise to my feet and raise the sword of the spirit high in the presence of your majesty and allow the glory of your word to radiate, dispelling the darkness first in me and as a beacon for all to see. My Lord, as I go forward with my eyes open wide, I ask that you use me and let thy will be done on earth as it is in heaven.

In the name of Jesus Christ my risen Lord and Savior, I pray.

Conclusions

We as Christian believers are all supposed to be soldiers. We are in the Lord's army. Do you know the game plan? Do you have all the equipment you need? Know that you are in a war, you have an enemy, so expect a battle.

Every morning and throughout the day when you are being tested and tried, picture yourself being surrounded by God's power and empowered by Jesus as he gives you strength through each part of the full armor of God.

It's not your traditional war, and in fact, most people don't believe in this kind of battle at all. It is not fought with laser-guided missiles or high-tech aerospace engineering. It is a spiritual war. It is not fought with weapons you can see. But it is real just the same. It was real to Jesus; the Bible is filled with examples of his spiritual battles. It was also real to the Apostle Paul, and in the book of Ephesians, he shows us how to fight our spiritual battles and have victory over our unseen enemy.

Here is a paraphrase of something Ray Stedman once said: "As Christians our lives are to be lived openly before all men, transparent, a spectacle unto the entire world. Christians are to be demonstrations of the truth."

How are you at being a demonstration of the truth?
_____
_____
_____

AUTHOR'S EXAMPLE: In previous pages, I have spoken of honesty in action and in mind. I attempt to be fair in all my dealings, from returning too much change given to me by a cashier to turning my head from things that are temptations of the mind. I always tell the truth and attempt to provide actions that imply that I am a Christ follower in all that I do.

The Battle Is the Lord's

[David, speaking to Goliath:]"Then all this assembly shall know that the Lord does not save with sword and spear; for *the battle is the Lord's,* and He will give you into our hands" (1 Samuel 17:47 NKJ).

"Hear, O Israel, today you are going into battle against your enemies. Do not be faint-hearted or afraid; do not be terrified or give way to panic before them. For the Lord your God is the one who goes with you to fight for you against your enemies to give you victory" (Deuteronomy 20:3–4 NIV).

"It is God who arms me with strength and makes my way perfect. He makes my feet like the feet of a deer; he enables me to *stand* on the heights. He trains my hands for battle; my arms can bend a bow of bronze. You give me your shield of victory, and your right hand sustains me; you stoop down to make me great" (Psalm 18:32–35 NIV).

"'Not by might nor by power, but by my Spirit,' says the Lord Almighty" (Zechariah 4:6 NIV).

"Because of Him, and through Him, and to Him are all things. To Him be the glory forever! Amen" (Romans 11:36 GLT).

Now that you know of the armor and the true location of the battle, what are you going to do, how are you going to do it, and when are you going to start?

_____
_____
_____
_____

I am going to attempt to study more deeply the word of God so that when the time comes, I will not only be armored, I will be ready to defend and take the attack to the source, whether it be mental or physical; therefore, I must be prepared through immersion in the word of God. I will attempt to lead a life in such a manner that will epitomize these core values of the warrior:

- Faith. I will believe in the power of the written word.
- Service. I will reach out to others in need and always look for ways to help.
- Unity. I will unite with my brothers in Christ to strengthen our resolve to serve our Savior Jesus Christ.
- Courage. I will seek the strength to change in me what needs to be changed and to accept that which I cannot.
- Honor. I will live my life in a manner that is not overbold but which seeks out truth and wisdom to use in service of others.
- Vision. I will attempt to cast a vision into the hearts and minds of those who wish to further their lives in service to help others.
- Duty. I will look for ways to serve others and thereby serve my Lord for the glory of God.

- Freedom. I will strive to help others to find freedom in forgiveness, from bondage to sin of all types, and to achieve personal freedom in all its forms.

Okay, so now you are feeling battle-ready, and you have on the full armor of God. Ask yourself a question: When does a sin begin? Is it when you have a sinful thought enter your mind, or when you choose to continue thinking on this thought? The answers lies within the difference between temptation and sin. You have no control over the temptations the devil puts in your path. Your response to temptation is either to redirect your thoughts to scripture or praise God (the best choices), or to carry the temptation into a daydream and fantasize about it (sin).

Keep a favorite Bible verse or gospel hymn close at heart. When tempted, start saying the verse or singing the hymn in your mind. The devil cannot stand for God to be praised, glorified, or worshiped because the devil wants these things for himself. The devil will flee the battle as you praise, glorify, or worship God.

Remember: The battle is ongoing, but Christ has already won the victory through his death and resurrection. Satan and his demons don't acknowledge Jesus' victory and will continue to fight for the mind and soul of mankind until Judgment Day.

Prayer in the Spirit

Prayer in the Spirit is an important, ongoing activity of spiritual warfare. Paul included it in his discussion of the whole armor of God in Ephesians 6:18: "Praying always with all prayer and supplication in the Spirit, being watchful to this end with all perseverance and supplication for all the saints," and Jude mentioned it in his epistle (20-21): "But you, dear friends, build yourselves up in your most holy faith and pray in the Holy Spirit. Keep yourselves in God's love as you wait for the mercy of our Lord Jesus Christ to bring you eternal life."

Your Role: There are two participants involved with prayer in the Spirit: the Holy Spirit and you. Your part is to pray always with all prayer and supplication in the Spirit and to be watchful with all perseverance and supplication for all the saints. This does not mean that you have to be on your knees all day and night, with eyes closed in prayer. Prayer in the Spirit is an inner activity of the mind and spirit, where you maintain a type of open dialogue with God through the Holy Spirit. Outward actions such as bowing the head and closing the eyes may help you focus better on God, but it's the inner communication with God that matters most.

In order to always be in prayer, you need to be in control of your thoughts. When your thoughts are stuck on sinful fantasies, it will be difficult, if not impossible, to be in prayer. This is one of the reasons why you are to use the spiritual weapons God gives you to continually be "casting down imaginations, and every high thing that exalteth itself against the knowledge of God, and bringing into captivity every thought to the obedience of Christ" (2 Corinthians 10:5).

The definition of "supplication" is asking for humbly or earnestly, as by praying. Prayer is an acknowledgment that you are not in control and need God to intervene. This attitude opens the door for communication with God, who can direct and apply your prayers in ways far beyond your understanding. Therefore, when you pray to God, you should do so earnestly, in humility, inviting the Holy Spirit to work in the situation as God wills. It is really that simple.

The Spirit's Role: Once you've prayed, the Spirit intercedes for you and pleads on your behalf according to God's will. Paul described how the Spirit intercedes in Romans 8:26–27: "So too the Holy Spirit comes to our aid and bears us up in our weakness; for we do not know what prayer to offer nor how to offer it worthily as we ought, but the Spirit himself goes to meet our supplication and pleads in our behalf with unspeakable yearnings and groanings too deep for utterance. And He who searches the hearts of men knows what is in the mind of the Holy Spirit, because the Spirit intercedes and pleads before God in behalf of the saints according to and in harmony with God's will."

Leaving prayer concerns in God's hands can be challenging if you're prone to being in control and think you know what God should do. Too often, prayer becomes you telling God what to do (i.e., praying your will instead of his will be done). In situations where God's will is unclear, you should take care not to presume his will. Praying in the Spirit doesn't require that you speak intelligible words, but simply that you lift up the situation to God and trust that the Holy Spirit will intercede perfectly for you.

What Prayer in the Spirit Accomplishes: There are some important things that happen when you pray in the Spirit. Specifically, prayer in the Spirit

- perfects your prayer (Romans 8:26),
- takes your case directly before God (Romans 8:27),
- increases effectiveness of prayer for others (intercessory prayer) (Romans 8:27), and
- aligns your prayer with God's will (Romans 8:26–27).

Now that you have studied each piece of the armor, here is a summary prayer that may be helpful for putting on the whole armor each day:

Heavenly Father, I praise and worship you because you are God. I am honored to be your servant, and I take my stand today against the devil and his schemes against my family, my ministry, and me. Father, as I take up each piece of armor, please secure it in place on me.

I shod my feet with the preparation of the Gospel of peace. I have peace with God through the blood of Jesus. I have favor with God and with man. I walk in my inheritance as an adopted child of God and have authority over evil in Jesus' name. "Father, prepare me by helping me know Jesus in a deeper way. Let your word become the guiding light for every step I take today and let the knowledge of the good news of Jesus' death and resurrection be my source of peace" (Romans 5:1).

I gird my loins with the belt of truth. Your word, O God, is truth. Father, sanctify me according to your word and remind me through the Holy Spirit of the truth that destroys the lies of sin. "Father, I commit myself to Jesus as the foundation of my life today. With your strength Lord, I will resist the temptation to stand on any worldly foundation. Jesus, you alone are my foundation for any situation that will arise today" (John 14:6).

I put on the breastplate of righteousness, which covers my body with the righteousness of God. In Christ, every foothold of evil has been washed away, and I am clothed in righteousness. "I can fight any battle today because of the righteousness of Jesus, not my own! Jesus I declare that you are my righteousness and that through the victory of the cross I can stand victorious against temptation, sin and the attacks of our enemy" (2 Corinthians 5:12).

I put on the helmet of salvation, which protects my mind from the enemy's attacks. I have the mind of Christ. "Jesus, you are my salvation. You are my deliverance. Deliver me from all sins and weaknesses—spiritual, physical, and emotional. Cover me with strength, peace and anointing and bring me to complete wholeness in you" (1 Thessalonians 5:8–9).

I take up the shield of faith and extend it over myself. It extinguishes all the fiery darts of the evil one. "Father, by faith, connect me to the power of Jesus. My desire is to trust in you and your strength alone. Protect me from the arrows of the enemy today as I rely on your power. Give me faith so I may go forward doing your will" (Hebrews 11:33–34).

I will take up the sword of the spirit, the powerful word of God, and use it by speaking the word of God as it applies to whatever situation I may face today. Father, please remind me of your word via the Holy Spirit. "Jesus, you are the living version of God's word. May God's Word give me wisdom to apply the Word to life's situations and today's troubles" (Hebrews 4:12).

We are at war. It's not your traditional war, and in fact, most people don't believe in this kind of battle at all. It is not fought with laser-guided missiles or high-tech aerospace engineering. It is a spiritual war. It is not fought with weapons you can see. But it is real just the same. It was real to Jesus; the Bible is filled with examples of his spiritual battles. It was also real to the Apostle Paul, and in the book of Ephesians, he shows us how to fight our spiritual battles and have victory over our unseen enemy. Therefore, I will continue to pray in the Spirit throughout the day and intercede for all Christians as the Holy Spirit prompts me. I believe that the Holy Spirit is interceding on my behalf according to my prayers.

So finally, picture yourself putting on the armor of God, starting with the **Sandals of Peace,** by exhaling fully and breathing in the peace of God. Invite the Holy Spirit to show you anyone with whom you need to be reconciled. Forgive them and seek your forgiveness. Next, wrap the **Belt of Truth** around your waist and ask Jesus to show you the truth about yourself. Ask for discernment to know God's leading from that of the evil one. Strap on the **Breastplate of Righteousness** to get right with God by confessing any sin. Invite Jesus to make you into his likeness. Since your mind is where the battlefield is, put on the **Helmet of Salvation** and reclaim and celebrate your salvation. Let Christ give you his mind and thoughts. To support your body armor, envision yourself picking up the **Shield of Faith** and extinguishing doubts and temptations. Now it is time to draw the mighty **Sword of the Spirit** and cut yourself free from anything that restricts you from living in faith and health. Let the word of God shine in and through you to allow you to become not only a warrior for Christ but also a light unto the world, a guide who will stand when others fall and lead where others fear to go. Let the Holy Spirit lead you in worshipping God and intercede for others God brings to mind.

Father God, every day, help me to remember to put on your armor. I need this armor to protect my mind from things that are not of you. I need it to guard my heart from acting on emotions rather than with your Spirit. I daily need it to remind myself that I am a child of yours and that I do not serve Satan. I need the armor to be an instrument of peace and not react with my old nature. Lord, let your words speak through me to those in darkness, penetrating the enemy and crushing his plans. In Jesus' name, Amen.

WARRIORS SHIELD

† ARMY OF †
GOD

The Warrior's Shield Defined

The outer shield is split into three sections: The top of the shield, above the crown, represents the battlefield of the mind, where most battles are fought, won or lost. This is the place where you cannot hide from yourself. The two side sections represent the world in which you live. It is split into two sections: one for good people and things in life, and the other for chaos, which seeks to conquer all.

The inner shield represents the warrior, who is placed between the two warring factions; he stands on God's word and power to defend the weak and destroy evil.

The crown of glory stands for God, who is your King. The placement at the top of the shield signifies that this is where God is in your life: above all things.

The crossed arrows stand for readiness for battle. The placement between the crown of glory and the dove of peace signifies that sometimes peace can only be achieved through war.

The dove of peace symbolizes the Holy Spirit. The placement above the primary circle is to remind you that as the Holy Spirit descended upon Jesus after his baptism in the waters of the Jordan, you too have been baptized in the Spirit.

The six swords stand for one of each of the pieces of God's armor. The placement of the swords on either side of the dove represents that you must be willing to fight for one another and that God has provided you with the weapons needed to do so.

The primary circle stands for the circle of life. This is at the center of the shield because it holds the peace through the sacrifice of Jesus and the relationship you now have with the trinity and the unity among your brothers in Christ, who are led by the Spirit.

PAX stands for Christ Jesus, who is the source, reconciliation, and peace. Jesus is at the center of life, for without his sacrifice, you would not be able to have eternal life and a relationship with God, who is your Father.

The Triquetra symbolizes the Trinity; this is located on the right side of the PAX, with the three points representing Father, Son, and Holy Spirit, while the continuous interwoven line represents unity.

The joined rings stand for brotherhood; this is located on the left side of the PAX, representing a rope made of many strands that will not be broken.

The wheel of hope is located at the bottom of the shield; it contains all that you want or hope to be. Your core values exemplify a character of excellence; they are who you already are and who you become during this incredible journey with our Father in heaven. These are the values:

- **Faith**: firm belief in something for which there is no proof; complete trust
- **Service**: contribution to the welfare of others; a helpful act
- **Unity**: continuity without deviation or change of purpose or action; the quality or state of being made one

- **Courage**: mental or moral strength to venture, persevere, and withstand danger, fear, or difficulty
- **Vision**: a dream, strongly desired goal, or purpose
- **Honor**: character, a good name, reputation; one's word given as a guarantee of performance; moral excellence and fairness
- **Duty**: binding of tasks, conduct, service, or functions that arise from one's position in life; the force of moral obligation
- **Freedom**: absence of necessity, coercion, or constraint in choice or action; liberation from slavery or restraint or from the power of another; independence

The hub located in the center of the wheel is to remind you that when you act in unison, you are of one mind, one heart, and one Spirit. This is the source of your reason to not accept failure.

The wheel is always moving forward and affords you the agility to spin about in defensive or offensive maneuvers. It contains eight spokes; each stands for one of your core beliefs upon which you cannot be shaken. The hub represents the weak: those for whom you are commissioned to stand for, to protect, and to defend. The spokes connect them to the living word of God.

The point of contact between the wheel and the circle represents the turning of your life, the point in which once and for all times, you have been saved through the blood of Christ. For without being connected to the primary circle of life, you cannot truly succeed at that which you hope to achieve.

There is a battle forming that is encompassing the world, one that is being fought on the physical, temporal, and spiritual planes of existence. This battle is between good and evil, in which no one will get out alive, yet in the middle stands the warrior. It is he who through wisdom, faith, and knowledge of the word of God puts his life on the line for the children of God, who are lost, misled, or alone.

This battle is not hiding in the shadows; it is in your life—your mind and heart. The enemy is doing his best to flank you if you're strong in Christ, to openly confront you if you are weak. He is the author of deception, and if you try to stand alone, he will distract you and overcome your defense, so stand united in a brotherhood of Christ and know that your back is protected.

Where do you see yourself?

Now at the beginning of this study, I told you I would share the prayer that I pray daily to renew the armor of God upon my body. I am never without this armor; on a daily basis, it receives its share of dents, dings, and tarnish, so I pray for renewal and the daily refurbishment from the trials, temptations, and sins that tear at my heart and mind regularly.

There are two parts to this prayer; one is for me, and the other is for those who are drawn into my sphere of influence through my interaction with life on a daily basis.

Prayer to Put on and Renew the Armor of God

Note: Pray on the armor one time, and then pray for the renewal of the armor daily. I do this because if you pray it on daily, that means that at some point, the armor has to come off. I will not be without the protection of the armor for even a second. So to pray it on, instead of asking the Lord to "renew me through the ____," pray "Lord, I put on the ___", then every day thereafter, pray the renewal.

Now Lord, I ask that you renew me through the armor of God upon my body so that I may follow where you lead and lead where you send me.

Lord, renew me through the sandals of peace upon my feet, so that I may walk upon the path you have placed me on, so that I may walk on, over, around, or through any obstacles or pitfalls placed there by the enemy. Renew me so that I may accept your peace in my life and that the turmoil that often afflicts me will be overcome, and your peace will reign in my life. Fill me with your peace, so that I may share your peace with others, in hope that they too may understand your love and forgiveness. I know that this peace does not mean that all things will be perfect, rather that you will help me through all that comes my way.

Lord, renew me through the belt of truth girded about my waist, for your word is truth, and truth is in your word. And help me to live a life of truth and to discern truth in all things so that I may better serve you in all that I do. And help me to share your truth with others.

Lord, renew me through the breastplate of righteousness upon my chest, so that I may stand in your righteousness, since I have none of my own. And protect my heart and help me to use love, compassion, understanding, and wisdom in all my dealings with others, and help me to temper my thoughts so that I am not self-righteous but compassionate in the way I treat others.

Lord, renew me through the helmet of salvation upon my head. I ask that you open my eyes to see, my ears to hear, and my lips to speak your words of praise, and that you will always be in the forefront of my mind at all times and in all things, to be my guide and my mentor. I ask that you protect my thoughts. And help me to uplift, edify, and encourage others.

Lord, renew me through the shield of faith upon my arm, to block the fiery darts of the enemy, protecting not only myself but others. I ask that you would grant me wisdom to use faith to bridge the gap between those who are lost and your son, Jesus, so that they too may one day have a relationship with our heavenly Father.

Lord, renew me through the sword of the spirit, your mighty and powerful word, for by your word, you created all things, you spoke life, and you spoke death. Teach me to wield this sword for your honor and glory and in service to you and for your children, so that I may use it in either defense or offence, to protect myself and others, and take the battle to the enemy when required. For this sword is your word of truth, and no power can stand against it.

The Warrior's Prayer

Note: Now that you have prayed on and are renewing the armor on a daily basis, take it a step further and offer yourself as a warrior for Christ.

Now Lord, I bow before you on bended knee and offer you my fealty and love, and I ask that you grant me serenity to accept the things I cannot change, the courage to change the things that I can, and the wisdom to know the difference.

Father God, I ask that you would bless me indeed and enlarge my territory, and that your hand would be with me to keep evil from me so that I may not be troubled by it or trouble others. And that you would help me to reach out to others in your name, and that you would grant me wisdom and discernment to follow your guidance in all things, and I pledge to you my allegiance for now and forever.

Now Lord, I rise to stand before you, a man dressed in your armor, a warrior preparing to go forth. And as I stand here, I cast my eyes to the heavens above and raise the sword of the Spirit on high in salute to you, my Lord, my God, and my King.

Lord, I ask that you would emblazon this sword with love, mercy, compassion, truth, wisdom, justice, strength, courage, and perseverance. And I ask that this light wash out, in, around, and through me, dispelling any darkness that may yet remain in me, and renew your armor upon my body. So that as I go forth, your light will precede me, banishing the darkness before me, revealing the enemy in its hiding places, driving them back into the netherworld from whence they have come.

Lord, I ask that you would reveal those who have been lost, broken, forgotten, and abandoned. And Jesus, you who are the light of the world, let your light shine like a beacon in the night so that they may come to you, so they too may have a relationship with you and the Father.

Jesus, so that I may bring honor and glory to the Father, I ask that you grant me wisdom like that of Solomon to love others and to discern truth in all things; grant me courage like that of David and Daniel to love others and not be afraid to show it, and to use everything at my disposal to further your word. And grant me humility like that of Moses, John, and Paul, to always know that it is not me but you working in and through me for God's glory.

For our struggle is not against flesh and blood, but against the rulers, against the authorities, against the powers of this dark world, and against the spiritual forces of evil in the heavenly realms. So Father, strengthen and aid me to be prepared by wearing your armor and become a warrior for you. So that now and when that day of evil comes, I will be able to stand my ground against the wiles of the enemy, stand firm, and stand in front of those who are unable to yet stand on their own.

You are my strength, my fortress, my refuge, and my God.

All this I ask and receive in the name Jesus, my Lord and Savior.

About the Author

Before coming to Christ, I thought of myself as not too bad of a person. I was brought up Roman Catholic and so believed in God and thought I would end up in heaven. Even so, my life was filled with self-serving things and actions. Sex, drugs, alcohol, and cursing were a part of my life, sometimes on a daily basis. As a child, I was ridiculed and picked on because I was fat, a momma's boy, and a son of the town drunk. From junior high through senior high school, I had few friends and was harassed by the local bullies. After high school, I enlisted in the U.S. Army and served for three years, where I changed and redefined who I was.

This is where I learned that I could take care of myself; I became what I considered a self-made man and started living by what I called the cowboy code. I believed in God but didn't think about him too much because the world became too interesting, and I became a product of a sinful nature. During this time, I did many things I am not proud of and even began to form a relationship with what I now know to be the enemy. I reveled in the freedom I thought I had when, in fact, I was becoming a slave to the corruption of alcohol, drugs, sex, and other worldly desires.

I still didn't think I was that bad of a person because I was now comparing myself to hardened criminals who belonged in prison. I failed to look back on my life to see that I too fell into the realm of those I perceived as criminal. At the age of forty-three,

I found Christ and received the salvation through his gift. I was washed in the blood of the Lamb and became born again into God's family. Now I know where I will go when my time on earth comes to an end. I now also know where the true battle lies. Before being saved (and even after), I was fighting a battle I didn't even know I was in. The war is being waged around us on a daily basis by those who are prepared and by those who are not. The war is in our streets, workplaces, businesses, even our homes and churches; the war is also in our hearts and minds.

The purpose of this study is not just to make others aware of the battles they are involved in (battles that encroach upon our every waking moments). It is also to help them to get prepared, to get armed, and to get armored. All battles throughout history involve preparation, planning, armament, and protection. These battles are fought in the physical world with physical weaponry. Jesus even talked to his apostles about becoming prepared and physically armed: "He said to them, 'But now if you have a purse, take it, and also a bag, and if you don't have a sword, sell your cloak and buy one'" (Luke 22:36). In the Old Testament, Isaiah tells us that God, in his displeasure with the lack of justice, prepared himself: "He put on righteousness as his breastplate, and the helmet of salvation on his head; he put on the garments of vengeance and wrapped himself in zeal as in a cloak" (Isaiah 59:17). God prepared himself to bring retribution to his foes, be they enemy nations or wicked Israelites. If God prepared himself for battle, what must we do to prepare for the battles we face? Know that we can't do it alone. Look about you; is the person sitting next to you at a restaurant, in the movies, or even in church prepared? How about the person standing next to you in line at a sports facility: Are they prepared? Do they even know about the war being waged around them as they walk through life? How about you yourself; are you aware, and if so, are you prepared? I know that I wasn't. Not until a fellow Christian, a member of my men's Bible study group, really read Ephesians

6:10–18 and asked, "What does this mean? Do we need to be prepared, and if so, how do we get prepared?" That was when I believe the Holy Spirit made his presence known and prompted me to answer this man's questions. I can't say that here in this study lie the answers to this battle we find ourselves in. What I can say is that through this study, we have become more aware of the battle and the manner in which the enemy carries it to us, as well as learning that we must prepare ourselves and how to work toward this preparedness. Those who go into battle unprepared will soon, to their own detriment, become a slave to the enemy or worse: vanquished in the wake of the enemy.

So let this study be a guide to open your eyes to see, your ears to hear, and your spirit to be fortified by the word of God. When the time arrives and you are called to stand, you can stand firm in the word of Christ, knowing that his truth will cover all Satan's lies.

"Be alert and of sober mind. Your enemy the devil prowls around like a roaring lion looking for someone to devour. Resist him, standing firm in the faith, because you know that the family of believers throughout the world is undergoing the same kind of sufferings" (1 Peter 5:8–9).

Printed in the United States
By Bookmasters